Published in 2022 by Yandara

First Edition

Yandara

Teaching Yoga from the Heart

By
Craig Perkins
and Aimee Hughes

Yandara Yoga Teacher Training
Baja California Sur, Mexico

Welcome to the Path

Teachers of yoga are intuitively tapping into something mysterious and profound: a transformational life force that is present within each and every one of us.

When we practice yoga we gain access to a wondrous system of physical movement that transforms us. Yoga changes our bodies. It changes our minds. It even touches our souls.

With a deep respect for the yoga tradition and a heartfelt intention for your work you can bring real health and happiness to your students. You can inspire. You can change lives. You can be this teacher. In fact, you will be this teacher because...

The path is graciously unfolding before you.

While most of us are aware of the transformative effects of yoga, do we really understand the how and why of its inner workings? New yoga teachers typically become inspired by a gifted mentor or teacher. They proceed to emulate their teacher's style in some way, in the hope of providing a similar experience for their own students.

However, without un[illegible] and why these results are achieved they [illegible] influences that create the beneficial exper[illegible] writings will explain in Western terms h[illegible] need to understand *all* aspects of yoga in [illegible] ers we can possibly be. We are endeavor[illegible] ce of body wisdom, awareness and sens[illegible] ent and queuing. We have developed this [illegible] rving what is most effective in terms of s[illegible] ffectively into poses that will be most benefi[illegible]

What is yoga?

The word *yoga* comes from the Sanskrit root word *yuj*, which means, *to join*.

But what is it that we're joining?

Yoga is a way of living that helps us join our individual self with a larger sense of life—the one that's outside ourselves. We might call it the universe, or consciousness, or the infinite. According to the original, classical yoga philosophy, the goal of yoga was exactly this—to connect the Atman (the soul) to Brahman (the ultimate reality underlying all phenomena).

But why would we want to do this? Why would we want to dedicate ourselves to a lifestyle in order to attain this particular union? Yoga teaches us that when we lose our limited sense of self and connect to a larger sense of self we live up to our highest potential. We live up to the highest sense of what's possible.

This is the purpose of yoga.

Yoga is the union between subject and object. It's the union between the small self and the timeless Self. It's also an ancient technology, a venerable philosophy, and a time-honored tradition. It's a truly vast philosophy and way of life with many different disciplines and paths.

This book is for yoga teachers who want to carry on this enduring tradition.

Over the past fifty years a vast number of varieties and brands of yoga have taken the Western world by storm—all created by teachers who have stamped their own personal signature on the classes they present. However, the essence of their classes come from the teachings of a very small group of original teachers from long ago. In the process of modernizing the ancient practice some basic aspects of it have been lost in translation.

In this book—which you'll be able to refer to again and again throughout your lifetime as a yoga teacher—we endeavor to answer some basic yet essential questions.

What is hatha yoga?

The Sanskrit word *hatha* means *force*. Therefore hatha yoga means *union through force*— through effort, exertion, and physical practice.

Hatha yoga involves physical movement practice. Whether the manner in which we move engages the muscles in a stationary way or in a rapid and repetitive one—whether it's dynamic or gentle—it's all part of hatha yoga.

To create something we refer to as life force energy, all we have to do is move the body: it's that simple. However, there are ways to move which are more efficient than others, and hatha yoga aims to move the body in the most efficient manner possible.

Every single movement impacts the life force energy of the body. As a yoga teacher, each movement you teach affects a specific part or area of the body. Therefore, you must always choose how you want to impact the bodies of your students. With that in mind, you then decide which postures to teach.

There's a principle of movement that states:

We gain the most benefit by moving the largest regions of the body first—spine, trunk and hips—followed by the smaller regions—shoulders, knees, elbows, and ankles.

This theory of movement is based on the notion that the health of the spine and major joints is essential to maintain overall health, and even longevity. Because, from a biological standpoint, we're just animals. To be a healthy animal, we must move our bodies.

Hatha yoga is inherently simple.

Hatha yoga is safe movement or engagement of muscles and connective tissues of the body performed in a state of presence, awareness, and positive energy.

At our core, we humans are a surprisingly adaptive species, and the underlying essence of an animal's existence is this:

If you don't use it, you lose it.

This is a biological concept illustrated by the adaptation of our journey as an evolving species. Humans are probably the most adaptive species on the planet. It's a compelling piece of information as we explore the yogic path.

Let's illustrate this further with the following scenario:

Imagine that the only thing you did all day, every day, was sit on a bench and lift weights. Your arms would grow very strong but the muscles in your legs would atrophy. This use it or lose it principle relates to the yoga practice in a rather exciting way. When we move the body with conscious awareness and with loving intention we create a life force that initiates growth, strength, and healing in the area upon which we put our focused attention.

Not unlike the basic principle of exercise, in which the body responds to repetitive movement by strengthening and adapting to the part of the body that's being moved, this principle, when applied to our yoga practice, creates health and healing in almost unfathomable ways.

What is prana?

The ancient healing traditions of yoga and Ayurveda, as well as the vast system of Chinese medicine, have long believed that we are energetic beings, composed of energy.

Thousands of years ago, yoga, acupuncture, tai chi, and qi gong developed a language to explain this concept, which goes something like this:

The human body is made up of nadis or meridians. Nadis are pathways through which an energy called prana (or *chi* in the Chinese tradition) flows. When we practice hatha yoga we move different parts of the body in order to harness this energy in the most effective manner. In doing so we're able to create a life force which heals and supports the body, mind and spirit in profound ways.

While many of these concepts and ideas are fairly new to Western science, studies done by orthopedic surgeon and bioelectricity pioneer Robert O. Becker have shown that moving the body in a relaxed way creates an electrical charge that stimulates growth in cells, improves overall health, and allows the ability of the organism to regenerate. Also, while in the past Western doctors would immobilize injured body parts in order for them to heal, in recent decades physical therapists have learned that effective rehabilitation requires movement. The body can't stay stagnant.

This mirrors what ancient yogis have been saying all along—movement heals. That's the whole premise here. A little electrical charge is created and this charge powers life.

The *use it or lose it* principle applies to humans, plants, and animals—all animate objects. It doesn't apply to inanimate objects, which on the surface seems apparent. But, delving deeper things get interesting. Living beings respond and react differently to life experiences when compared to non-living things. This is important to understand when we talk about the amazing benefits of yoga. My inspiration for this connection comes from the work of Paul Grilley, a yoga teacher whose articles and books all aspiring teachers should study.

Here's an example to illustrate this difference:

If you walk with a walking stick over a long period of time along concrete or pavement, the bottom of the stick will gradually wear down. Continue walking and eventually the stick wears down completely. But let's say you're walking along a sidewalk with bare feet. You walk barefoot for as long as you walk with that walking stick. Maybe even longer. If you walk slowly and don't overdo it, it has a healthy effect on your body; the soles of your feet get stronger.

But here's the thing: if you walk too fast or haphazardly, you'll wear out your feet, just like the stick. This is a crucial point for understanding healthy bodily movement. When you walk slowly and with gradual intensity over a period of months, the soles of your feet will calcify and strengthen. Unlike the stick that would have worn out long ago, your feet become stronger and more capable of walking long distances—barefoot.

What an amazing phenomenon for all living beings! How amazing! How mysterious!

When we walk, we rhythmically engage and release, or contract and relax. Through this rhythm, we create movement, which in turn, creates a life force. This life force runs along our energetic pathways and it regenerates the body. Allowing life force to flow along these nadis creates incredible bodily health.

Safety in our yoga practice

Safety is key when it comes to creating effective yoga sequences. As teachers, we need to keep ourselves free from injury. We also need to prevent injury for our students.

There are some safety fundamentals that we all need to understand clearly in order to teach with efficacy. By using specific fundamental movement principles in our teaching—rather than copying sequences we've learned, or approaching our instruction solely from a perspective focusing only on external alignment—we'll become the best yoga teachers we can possibly be.

All you're trying to do is create ways to affect different joints, muscles, and ligaments through movement. This movement allows prana to move more effectively through the body. As a yoga teacher, that's an important part of what you're doing.

When it comes to safety your students are their own best teachers and you're their guide. You make suggestions for safe postures. You help them find variations of the postures which create strong sensations in their bodies without causing pain or injury. Only your students can answer the question, "does this position cause pain?"

If the answer is yes, it's not yoga.

Pain simply means a particular pose isn't working for your student, so you gently guide them out of it. That's all.

Let's illustrate this further:

If I lift my arm as straight and as high as possible, while totally extending my shoulder joint, I can tell you when and where the pain begins. I feel when sensations become a bit too intense. So, I back off a bit. It's about finding one's personal edge. *This* is intuitive yoga. As an intuitive yoga teacher, this is where you guide your students—to that sweet spot—the one that hovers on the edge but never goes beyond it. You take your students to this place in a completely present and loving way.

Intuitive yoga is about being able to distinguish between a sensation that grabs your attention and a sensation that's clearly too much. You can ask your students to diagnose their own sensations, to differentiate between sensations that challenge, and those that cause pain or harm. To be a great yoga teacher, you'll want to teach your students how to safely create beneficial sensations in every posture.

While this *self-diagnosis* concept seems simple, in some cases, it's complex. And as yoga teachers we're responsible for understanding these complexities. So let's delve deeper.

If it hurts, it's time to back off.

When you give your students this instruction, what do you mean exactly? Do your students know what pain feels like in their bodies? Some will but some won't. And for those who don't, how do you teach them how to recognize pain? Because somewhere along the way you'll come across a student who is so disassociated from their own body that they no longer know how pain truly feels. In your future teaching years you may have numerous students come to class completely off-balance and living in a state of chronic stress and out of touch with the sensations of their body.

As an intuitive yoga teacher you have the tools to teach your students how to become embodied. You can help them leave states of constant stress behind. What a gift!

By helping your students find ways to determine where their individual threshold for pain lies you give them the priceless gift of getting to know their bodies. This is perhaps the most important skill to teach your students—how to tune in and connect to their own bodies.

Here is a practice that may help your students learn to evaluate when a sensation is too much. Simply stand on one leg. Feel how long you can stand on one leg before it gets to be too much, then switch legs. Some students will change legs very quickly. Others will last longer depending upon their bodies. Eventually, everyone's standing leg begins to tire and contract. A little bit of pain arises. After a while, students recognize how surprisingly intense these sensations are. They think: *Wow! I started and thought I could go on forever.* Two minutes in and—*this is too much!*

By teaching this exercise you allow your students to become familiar with their body's way of saying, *this is too much.* Experimenting with our edge is necessary for self-diagnosing painful sensations—both on and off the mat.

Another aspect of safety in the poses involves our natural inclination to compete. While comparing and competing is commonplace in our society, it isn't a part of yoga. Yoga is *not* a competition: it's the furthest thing from a competition. As teachers we should remind our students of this again and again. Problems can arise when we compare ourselves to others. I've gone to yoga classes—especially partner yoga classes—where you can't help but want to keep up with everyone. So you might push too hard and hurt yourself.

Sure, push yourself a little—but not until it hurts. As a general rule, yoga should not induce pain. It's not a competition. Ingraining this concept into your students' awareness is fundamental for leading safe and effective classes. You might end up sounding like a broken record—but that's what it takes for new information to sink in. So say it over and over again.

If what you are doing on your mat brings you pain, it's not yoga.

As intuitive yoga teachers we need to continually remind our students to tune into their bodies, to constantly bring them back, again and again, to the sensations they're experiencing in the moment. Where *is* that place that's not too much—and yet not too little? One of our best sleuthing tools is the *Goldilocks and the Three Bears Policy.* We find those *not too much and not too little, but just right* sensations.

Encourage your students to become aware of sensations several times during class, to find the sensations that are *just right* for them in any given pose. Even regular and advanced students need this reminder. Our bodies are different each time we come to class. They're constantly in flux. Thus, the poses from yesterday will inadvertently feel different today. Those edges will be in different places, too. What once felt like too much might now feel just right. And what felt just right last week might feel downright painful today. This is why we continually check in with our bodies. Through the lens of our magnifying glass we scrutinize each sensation with patience and curiosity.

What a good lesson in managing expectations this is! There's no need to expect your body to master the pose it mastered yesterday or last week. And just because you're able to balance on one foot without falling during class today it doesn't mean tomorrow will hold the same story. When expectations aren't met, and some days they won't be, resist the urge to be competitive—even with yourself.

As you can see, sensation cues are a necessary tool to use while teaching intuitive yoga classes.

The science behind intuitive yoga

Our bodies are so intelligent, and if we pay attention to them we'll prevent injury and promote healing during any and every form of movement. Let's take an example relevant to teaching yoga: stretching.

Muscle contractions are a bodily response associated with protection. Stretch receptors within your muscle fibers, called muscle spindles, keep track of how much tension is created in a muscle at any given moment. If you stretch a muscle too quickly or too much, the muscle spindle causes the muscle to contract (or shorten) in order to prevent injury.

It's a natural reflex built into every muscle fiber in your body. If you pay close attention to your body as you move, you'll find it difficult to create pain. Before pain even happens, your muscles contract to protect you. This is especially noticeable in weak spots and areas of your body that have been injured in the past.

Let's say you have a history of lower back pain. You're really careful with your lower back during yoga because you're scared you might injure it. If you've experienced pain in even the simplest of postures before, your muscles will contract to protect that area if you begin to move into the pose that previously caused pain. This remembering is something your body does to protect you and prevent previous traumas from happening again. While this is good in some ways it limits you in others. In fact, it can become an obstacle to healing through movement.

Somatic memory, also known as muscle memory, is information that's stored in the body. It's impossible to use your mind or willpower to override these memories because your body knows otherwise. Those issues have become deeply embedded in your tissues. Evidence of this comes to the surface when muscles contract out of fear, even before you've gone fully into the posture. It's as if the body believes it's about to experience pain before pain even occurs.

One of hatha yoga's goals is to avoid involuntary muscle contraction. Every posture we enter is meant to create harmony in the body through stability and relaxation. We contract the muscles that are necessary and beneficial to contract and let the rest of the body remain relaxed. When we teach yoga we're helping our students' bodies open up to movement that promotes stability and relaxation. Blood circulates, nerves release tension, and energy moves freely. For all this to occur the body must be at ease. It cannot be in a state of stress or habitual contraction.

While we've defined yoga as *any* form of movement, some postures and movements are intrinsically challenging. The question is this:

How do we teach our students to *relax* into these postures as they maintain the stability to hold or move through them?

To answer this question, we explore exertion. How hard should we be working in each pose? We typically think 80-95% capacity is necessary to reap the purported benefits of physical exercise. But yoga is different. Yoga is all about finding that sweet spot, remember? Not too much, not too little. It's at this point where we achieve the many benefits of our yoga practice.

As yoga teachers this is something we need to teach in each class, while also reminding our students that the sweet spot is going to look and feel different in each body. Yoga celebrates our uniqueness, and this is yet another example where we celebrate the many changes that happen in our bodies from one moment to the next—from person to person. It's crucial to reiterate this point again and again to keep your students safe and consistent in their practice, while reaping the many rewards of yoga.

For some students—especially those coming from an exercise background—a balanced yoga practice might not seem like enough. Remind them that we want the practice to be sustainable so that it can be maintained for a lifetime. Exercising at a high intensity level can break your body down over the years, while yoga builds and preserves it.

To help this point sink in, you might consider using the walking stick analogy in class. The feet gradually grow stronger as we walk on them repeatedly and over an extended period of time. If you push too hard too soon, the tissues of the feet will wear down. Our bodies naturally respond positively to moderate activities, or to the balance between activity and rest. The sweet spot approach is a way to help students learn how to find their own healthy edge in a yoga pose. It is where we create powerful sensations in our body without wearing it down.

Alignment

"Lengthen the spine and elongate the neck."

"Maintain the wrists directly below the shoulders."

"Draw the low ribs back."

"Keep a slight bend in the knees."

"Feel into the lines of energy pulsating throughout your body."

Ever heard any of these phrases in a yoga class? They're used all the time, all over the world. Why? Because they speak to the subject of alignment. As you probably know, making sure your students practice good alignment within a pose is an integral part of being an effective yoga teacher.

Alignment is inherently important and beneficial for a myriad of reasons. Good alignment in a yoga pose enhances energy flow throughout the body. It helps us experience yoga with greater ease and fluidity of movement. When we have a practice that embodies proper alignment we're far less likely to get injured while practicing.

But first things first: let's define the term alignment. What is it exactly? Alignment is the balance between two opposing forces. In yoga asana practice, it means the precise positioning of the body in a particular pose—one that prevents injury while also giving the body maximum benefit. Some teachers use props to help students with alignment while others don't. Some teachers make alignment the focus of class while others barely mention it.

Some styles of yoga, such as Iyengar Yoga, holds alignment as a primary focus. In other, more flowing styles, such as vinyasa yoga, it is more challenging for the teacher to delve deeply into alignment principles. Some alignment instructions are contradictory from one instructor to the next. If this happens, just ask questions. It's important that you understand alignment principles well so that you can help your students understand them, too.

Here are some alignment principles to keep in mind while teaching any kind of hatha yoga class:

- Begin by aligning the foundation of a pose. In a standing posture, for example, properly placing the feet will prevent stress on the knees and hips.
- Stack the joints. Stabilizing the joints in all poses fosters safety and support for the entire body.
- Breath can be used to foster good alignment. With each inhalation focus on elongating the spine, and with each exhalation draw the navel in and up to engage the core.

- The risk of injury is often greater during transitions into or out of a pose. By being mindful and using the breath to transition we're less likely to injure ourselves.

Yoga practice is meant to help us experience freedom, joy, and a deep sense of well-being. Getting injured because of poor alignment will hinder this enjoyment. Good alignment principles help us experience all that yoga has to offer.

The yoga of intent

So what's the point of all this? What's the point of activating a radiant life force through movement? And if yoga is essentially any position the body can move through, how is it different from a step class or a jog around the block? What's the difference between chaturanga and plank and, say, a push-up? How is it more than just a culturally different take on physical fitness? From the periphery—not much. But, go deeper, and chaturanga becomes much more than just a push-up.

The difference between yoga and good old-fashioned exercise is the *intent* placed on the movement, as well as the energy the movement creates. Thoughts, sounds, and feelings associated with yoga all make it different from conventional exercise too.

Imagine your gym teacher barking:

Okay, now drop and give me twenty! Come on, five more! You got this! Now, do it! How does this make you feel? Some people are used to it. Maybe, it's a little exciting to be pushed with such fervor, but it's undeniably jarring. And the experience is primarily external. You're not internalizing your body's sensations at all. It can also be aggressive, and even shocking to the system.

Japanese scientist Masaru Emoto's well known photographs of water crystals present a profound notion of the effect intent may have on reality.

His famous experiment involves the idea that thoughts and intentions can actually *change* the appearance of individual water crystals, with positive loving words and thoughts creating beautiful, symmetrical crystals and negative, unpleasant words and thoughts creating ugly and malformed crystals.

You can find information about the Emoto experiments on the internet. And while it's yet to be proven whether his experiments show conclusive proof of what many people naturally intuit, it's intriguing to think about the implications – especially when we consider that the human body is made up of about 60% water. We *are* water, and many of us have had the experience of picking up on the vibe in a room, or from a particular person – whether for better or for worse. It's very possible that our physical bodies are responding to the thoughts and intentions of others. And, of course, as many scientific experiments have shown, our health and the state of our being is directly affected by *our own* conscious thoughts and intentions.

This is the difference between yoga and exercise. When we move within a space filled with consciousness, grace and presence, we alter the internal structure of our own health. Our body heals itself. Yoga creates this for people.

That's the difference.

Teaching yoga is about creating a conducive space for your students, transforming themselves as they breathe and move. When you're conscious of your body while moving you create a life force, a field of energy that has a healing effect. When you're distracted and your attention is elsewhere, this healing effect eludes you.

This is especially true when you're moving in such an intense way that all you can think about is how much you wish it was over. This type of movement is not conducive to deep-level healing. Yoga asana, by contrast, roots itself in consciousness, which is why meditation is so closely linked to asana. Meditation establishes presence and clarity. It creates radiance and inner peace. Through asana practice and meditation, master yogis have learned to radiate such peace that they actually transform the world around them.

I once studied under a yogi who demonstrated this ability by creating the biggest miracle I'd ever seen in yoga. I was in Chicago, with hundreds of people attending his program—all of us staying at the O'Hare Hilton. The hotel's vibes left me feeling uncomfortable—I felt a stressful energy permeating it. It was also located where two highways intersect, with planes flying over.

I thought, *this is not an ideal setting for a program of yoga.* When my teacher, Darshan Singh arrived, I worried. How would he work in such a difficult environment? But within twenty-four hours his energy had transformed the entire hotel into something entirely different. It was exquisite and beautiful. Everyone was calm, warm, and welcoming. Being there felt like being enveloped in a constant hug.

For me, this was proof of yoga's true transformational power. This is how we create our health. It's what happens when we move ourselves within a field of energy that makes us feel good. It affects us on a deep-seated level and creates positive change. A subtle transformation is working within the body even if it's not apparent after every class.

The reason students return to yoga again and again is because of this—not necessarily because the teacher is particularly gifted in anatomy or physiology, but more likely because the teacher made them feel a certain way—connected. People often return to class because they feel inspired. And this feeling has the power to transform individuals, their health, and the world in which they live.

Let go of stress through breath, mindfulness, and heart-centered awareness

As a teacher, how do you inspire your students in subtle yet profound ways? Can anyone do this? The thought of being someone who invokes feelings of peace and presence may seem out of reach. Your mind will tell you you're not ready. You don't know enough yet. Your practice isn't perfect. You can't do every pose. Thoughts of self-doubt go on and on. And they plague us all. They are part of being human.

You worry people might not like you or that you'll say something stupid. Be aware that this is your mind talking. But *you* are not your thoughts. In reality, you're totally capable, in this moment, of being an extraordinary yoga teacher. You have everything it takes to inspire people. It comes from a place deep inside you, and it's available right here and now.

In order to access this place of peace and presence within we must learn to undo some things. First and foremost, we want to address the things that cause us negative stress. This type of stress is the first thing we undo. This happens through the practices associated with an intuitive yoga teacher training—asana, mindfulness, meditation, pranayama, and the cultivation of an open heart. Sure, there's work involved in undoing attachments to stress, but it can certainly be done.

Let's face it, life these days is challenging. It's stressful. Over time, this stress compounds in our emotional bodies if we don't have the tools to release it. Yoga is the perfect means of reducing stress in the moment—and continually, throughout our lifetime. As a yoga teacher your ability to help people let go of stress is one of the greatest gifts you'll be sharing with the world, because stress is the *number one* killer in the Western world. It's responsible for the majority of our illnesses, diseases, and everyday discomforts.

In a state of prolonged stress our bodies secrete a hormone called cortisol. The sympathetic nervous system kicks in as we tense up and become vulnerable to every external stimuli around us. It's as if we're *sympathetic* to everything in our environment. When this happens, the body doesn't absorb nutrients optimally. Inflammation ensues, impacting all the systems of the body.

I have used Paul Pearsall's Stress Test to illuminate for our students whether or not the level of stress at which they normally function is within a healthy range for their body. Traditionally used for patients with heart disease or those experiencing early signs of heart issues, the test says a healthy level is below ten. (The scale goes up to 100.)

Most of the results from those that take the test come in around 30 to 60. The lowest results typically come in at 25. Needless to say, we can do better. A safe score on the test is around 8-10. What a stressed out society we live in! What's worse, we've adapted to it. We consider this stressed out state of consciousness to be normal. In reality, it's not.

To reduce chronic stress the first step is to develop an awareness around it—by taking this stress test, for example, to see where you stand. As with anything, identifying the issue is the first step. The second step is to take action and find methods of healing. This is where our yoga and meditation practice enters the picture. But first, let's take a look at what stress is, and how it takes root in the body.

To understand stress we need to talk about the amygdala—a part of the brain most commonly associated with fear and the fight-or-flight response. In rare and threatening situations, the fight-or-flight response keeps us alive. But, it also keeps us from living courageously, from our hearts, because it often cannot tell the difference between real danger (the tiger chasing us in the African savannah) and perceived danger (beginning a new journey as a yoga teacher).

The amygdala also stores emotional memory, emotional trauma, and past residues of hurt and heartbreak. Then we have our hearts, yet another place that holds hurt and heartbreak. Our hearts have been broken open, time and time again. The amygdala says, "being open is dangerous. Avoid your heart. Move to your head. That's where you're safe." In order to access the heart and live from its intelligence we need to rewire and shape-shift the amygdala.

The fight-or-flight response protects us from dangerous situations, it is one of our most primal instincts. It resides in our subconscious and protects us—no matter what.

Let's take an example of how this works:

Imagine a toddler, exploring the family kitchen. She accidentally touches a hot stove. Her amygdala automatically kicks in and tells her that because the stove is hot, and has caused her pain, it's dangerous. The next time she finds herself near the stove, she instinctively pulls away. It's not necessary for her brain to say to itself, "Yesterday I was burned by putting my hand on a stove so I'll avoid doing that today." A toddler isn't able to think this way. Plus, the response needs to be faster than these thoughts in order to prevent getting burned. When she was burned, it happened *fast.*

See how our human consciousness develops? The toddler's immediate response in pulling away from the hot stove the second time around reflects this path of development through human consciousness.

You can see how valuable the fight-or-flight response is for us. I remember an incident in my own life when I nearly drowned. As I made it back to the beach my heart was pounding relentlessly. The experience was deeply traumatic. The next day as I was sitting quietly on the beach, looking in the opposite direction to the water, a wave touched my fingers. I jumped. I didn't see it and I didn't understand my overly dramatic reaction. I just reacted.

That would have never happened before the trauma. This is exactly what the amygdala does. Instinctively and blindly it says, *water—dangerous.* As you might imagine, it took me a while to be comfortable getting in the water. I had a clenching up sensation whenever I did, which was an instinctive and subconscious reaction—in severe cases it can be impossible to override. But in time, it can be done.

While this reflex mechanism is necessary for us to survive in the world, the amygdala has not evolved in stride with modern society. This is one of the most apparent reasons for much of the emotional turmoil and dilemmas and stresses that we have in our lives. The amygdala is so overwhelmed with information that it can't sort out what's really going on. So it can happen that every time a person sees water, they move into stress mode.

Here's an example of how this works:

A father and his little boy and girl are off to the park for a pleasant afternoon. Brother and sister have a little wooden boat which they push back and forth across the pond. Then, for whatever reason, the little boy picks up the boat up and runs away with it. He's just being a kid. The little girl chases after her brother. Then, she trips and falls and scrapes her knee, which bleeds a bit. Dad rushes over to console and soothe the little girl.

The following week finds the little girl at the park with her dad once again. This time she's with her best friend and they're playing at the pond with the little wooden boat. All of a sudden, the little girl's friend picks up the boat to empty it of water because it's not floating so well. The little girl instinctively, and for no apparent reason, runs over and hits her friend for picking up the boat. Dad comes over and scolds her for hitting her friend.

The little girl was triggered when she saw her friend picking up the boat because it reminded her of what her brother did the previous week. Her amygdala warned her, "This is dangerous" and she reacted instinctively, trying to prevent the same trauma from happening again.

And, of course, the young girl didn't understand what was really happening. She couldn't consciously look at everything that was going on. In this case, she overreacted. The following week when dad says, "Do you want to go to the park?" what does she say? "No, not today." And the little girl doesn't understand why she doesn't want to go to the park, it's her amygdala doing the talking. Now she just has an instinctive fear that going to the park is dangerous.

"Do you want to go to kindergarten?" Her mother asks one day. But all the kids are mean to her so that's a scary place, too. She responds, "No, I don't want to go." So her mother asks, "Then do you want to go home?" Home is no good either because mommy and daddy fight all the time and brother is mean to her. Life at this point feels sadly precarious.

This story gives us a clear understanding of what some aspects of our lives are really about. It feels as if everywhere we go, and everywhere we turn, we're in dangerous territory. This is what the amygdala does. It finds ways to protect us.

Fast-forward and that little child is twenty-one. She's simply trying to survive, as most of us are. Two young men want to marry her. One of them has a boat. The other one is a real bum—no good for her at all. The guy with the boat, however, is a man of integrity. Guess who she chooses?

Her amygdala is so overwhelmed with information that all it can do is associate boats with pain and danger. So she chooses the one that may not be good for her. She doesn't look at him with knowing eyes and a truth with the wisdom of her heart. Instead, she simply lives in reactivity and has no idea why.

She makes up excuses and says, "oh, Johnny with the boat? Not my type." It's important to see how this works for us, and how it's a basic problem in our lives. What we need to do is establish an awareness of our amygdala. Again, we need to be Sherlock Holmses of our being, asking the question: *What does my amygdala react to*? This may seem like a long and drawn out explanation in relation to yoga—but you'll see why it's so important as we venture on in our explorations of yoga and its deeply healing and transformative effects.

We need to study Maslow's hierarchy of needs in order to better understand why the amygdala reacts the way it does. Biologically speaking, we're mammals—animals programmed to survive. For survival we need physical safety. If we're in a burning building the amygdala will say: *Get the heck out!* If we're starving, we'll find ways to get food—at any cost.

If we're about to freeze to death, we certainly won't be thinking about work troubles or the boyfriend who just left us. We'll find ways to get warm. This is Maslow's hierarchy of survival needs. Once your survival needs are met you might start considering how lonely you feel or how your boss really ticked you off.

Next, we have emotional requirements. As mammals, we also need emotional nurturing. A baby suffers mentally if she doesn't receive proper emotional nurturing as a newborn. We have a human need to be held, to be nurtured, and to make safe connections with our mother. Once all of our survival needs are met, we seek companionship.

As we move up Maslow's hierarchy of needs we come to self-worth. All humans need a sense of self-worth and a sense of identity. If you're part of a family where your father continually tells you, *you're no good because you get lousy grades at school,* this is going to negatively impact your sense of self-worth. Our amygdala makes a note of this in its little journal of fear and feels unsafe in situations where self-worth is constantly diminished.

This is a survival mechanism that isn't easy to override, especially for children. It even becomes a part of who we are. As adults we gain a more truthful bird's eye view of what's really going on, but it still takes awareness. We may realize that, "Oh, my father constantly puts me down because he was abused as a child, and now he's just taking it out on me." Or: "mother's having a bad hair day, and that's why she snapped at me when I was chewing gum with my mouth open." We can reason this out. But as children we can't, so it's incredibly stressful for us.

Still, even as conscious and understanding adults our inner-child lives within us, and if we want our inner-child to be healthy we have to learn to see our triggers for what they are—old habitual ways of being. Learn to love your inner-child—and the inner-children of your students—holding space for whatever emotions need to surface. Being in this loving energy field heals. It's as simple as that.

The undoing of stress through asana

Luckily, we have tools that help us let go of stress, drop into our hearts, and master our survival patterns. We no longer need to be held captive by our biological determinism.

Through yoga asana we move our bodies in a way that brings our attention to the present moment. This is where we become aware of bodily sensations that live in the present moment. Our hearts also live and breathe present moment awareness, whereas the past and future are of the mind. The present moment is very real and empowering. When we're in the present moment we're in the energetic space of the heart. We feel love and passion. Passion and love don't exist in your brain, they exist in your heart. When we're deeply rooted in the present moment stress naturally melts away.

As we let go of stress through yoga, let's reiterate this:

We don't want to cause pain for ourselves or for our students.

Pain causes stress. Anytime we're uncomfortable or freaking out about something that feels overwhelming, we're stressed. Yoga is meant to help us de-stress. We want to move our bodies in ways that are healthy. This may be hard to recognize at times, because we're not really attuned to our bodies: we don't truly know the difference between pain and healthy challenge.

Let's also address the moment we begin to feel initial sensations. We all have a range of how much sensation we can take, and every yoga posture contains a range of sensations. There's a minimum kind of sensation and a maximum kind of sensation. Begin looking for the minimum sensation. Challenge yourself to see if you can feel something. Be with that and see if you can accept it. See if you can accept it as "just a sensation," even if it means a little bit of discomfort.

See if you can work through that. See if you can move onto the next level of sensation. Does that initial feeling, which may be a little uncomfortable, begin to feel okay? As you gradually work with these sensations you can move a little bit more, and a little bit more—until you find your threshold. You want to find the threshold of challenge without stress. Pay attention, because this threshold is very subtle.

When you're worried about something you don't even notice that your body's in pain. On the flip side, when you're completely present to the sensations of the body, you won't hurt yourself.

All that said, this is what I want for you:

I want you to be empowered as a yoga teacher. I want you to think and feel this:

If I can move my students' attention into their bodies then I can teach them to tune into where they're holding onto stress. If I can do that without hurting them, by simply making them aware of the present moment, and by tuning into sensations of discomfort and their individual thresholds for it, then I can teach effective yoga classes.

De-stress with the breath

One of the most powerful aspects of yoga is the way we pay attention to, and work with our breath. We study how and why the breath affects our mind, body, and spirit. We do this experientially, through breathwork known as pranayama. Pranayama techniques have a number of healing benefits and they're an integral part of the yoga tradition, which is why it's a good idea to include at least one breathing technique in each yoga class we teach. Let's take a look at a handful of those breathing practices now.

Humming Bee breath

One of the more humorous pranayama techniques you could teach is called humming bee breath. The name for it in Sanskrit is bhramari. I like humming bee breath because when we imitate an animal or do something a little bit goofy or out-of-the ordinary we immediately become lighter. We don't take ourselves so seriously. And that's always a good thing to practice during a yoga class.

Health benefits of humming bee breath run the gamut. It helps with sleep issues, thyroid problems, sinus issues, and anxiety. It also quiets the mind to help us drop into our heartspace. The gentle buzzing sound we make helps switch on the parasympathetic nervous system, thereby calming our minds and bodies.

To practice humming bee breath:

1. Inhale deeply.
2. Now exhale slowly and, as you do, create a low-pitched humming sound from your throat. Allow the sound to permeate your brain until you're out of breath.
3. Then, inhale again, and repeat. Close your eyes, cover your ears, and *let go.*

Ujjayi breath

Ujayii translates to *victorious.* It's the most beloved breath in our world of yoga, and one that you'll teach again and again. It's simple, too. We use ujjayi breath throughout a yoga class, unless we're specifically practicing another pranayama technique.

1. Sit comfortably, close your eyes, and soften your gaze.
2. Begin to breathe as you naturally would. Your mouth is closed, although you could part your lips gently.

3. Deepen your inhale through the nose and bring it to the back of your throat at the top of the inhalation.
4. As you exhale, push the breath from the roof of your mouth, making an ocean sound.

The nose is the doorway for ujjayi breath, but the action comes from the back of your throat. You'll be able to hear it, but your neighbor needn't. That's a good gauge for volume.

Ujjayi breath focuses the mind and brings it back to the task at hand—great for bringing attention back to the present moment. If you're feeling tired, elongate the inhalation. If you're feeling anxious, lengthen the exhalation.

Alternate Nostril Breathing

One of the most popular pranayama practices, nadi shodhana, is said to balance the masculine and feminine aspects of ourselves. The left nostril is associated with the feminine moon/chandra energy, and the right nostril is associated with the masculine sun/surya energy.

1. Sit comfortably with your left hand on your knee, in gyan mudra, or whatever feels good.
2. Cover your right nostril with the right thumb, while the ring finger rests on the left nostril. Your pointer and middle fingers rest on your forehead, or third eye center.
3. Press on the right nostril to close it off, while inhaling through the left. At the top of the inhale, close off the left nostril, exhaling through the right.
4. Now, inhale through the right nostril, then press down on the right nostril as you exhale through the left. This completes the 4-part circle, balancing out both sides.

When to use it: When you need to balance anything—masculine and feminine, thoughts or actions—come to this breath.

4-Count Breath/Box breathing

This is a great pranayama technique because of its simplicity. It's also great for anxiety relief—when you're stressed out or upset about something. It goes like this:

1. Find a comfortable seated or supine position. Exhale all the breath out.
2. Inhale through your nose for a count of 4.
3. Hold the breath for a count of 4.
4. Exhale for a count of 4.
5. Hold the breath for a count of 4.
6. Repeat.

Easy, right? You might instruct your students to close their eyes as they do this, and even blow the exhale out of the mouth for a more cooling effect.

When to use it: Perfect for relieving stress and anxiety, or when you simply need to slow down the pace of whatever you're doing and drop into the moment.

Kapalabhati (Skull Shining)

This is a dramatic breath with short, strong, forceful exhalations and short, passive inhalations. Your diaphragm is the powerhouse behind these staccato-like movements.

1. Make two fists with your hands, with the thumb side pressing lightly into your belly. Inhale and exhale deeply.
2. Take a short inhale and then begin making short, forceful exhalations out of your nose while pumping from your diaphragm. You'll naturally inhale as you do this but place your attention on the staccato exhales.
3. Practice this for 1-3 minutes.

When to use: When you want to see things with greater clarity.

Nasal breathing

To simply breathe in and out of the nose has a powerful impact on the nervous system and helps us heal in all sorts of amazing ways. When we breathe in and out through our nostrils the air is filtered and humidified, making it easier for the lungs to use. Nasal breathing also produces *nitric oxide*. Nitric oxide is a vasodilator that helps to widen the blood vessels, which, in turn, can lower blood pressure and increase blood flow in the body.

Nasal breathing may feel strange at first, because many of us breathe through the mouth. But once you start practicing nasal breathing you'll feel how relaxed you become. It's a really healing way to breathe once you get used to it. Ayurveda teaches nasal breathing during exercise as a form of disease prevention.

Once you familiarize with nasal breathing you can even sleep with a very light piece of tape over your mouth at night to ensure you're breathing in and out of the nose. Many people report a deeper, more restorative sleep; they wake up feeling more energetic and rejuvenated, as well as calmer and more mentally alert. Encourage your beginner students to try nasal breathing, even for parts of the yoga class, and then build on it from there. Eventually, all breathing is done through the nose during asana practice.

Add relaxing aromatherapy to your yoga classes

One of the most creatively therapeutic ways to alleviate stress is to integrate the art of aromatherapy into your yoga practice and classes. Aromatherapy is a healing art of ancient origins which uses the essences or essential oils of plants to heal the body and mind. Essential oils are the origins of medicine as well as the origins of perfume. In India, this aromatic tradition has been a part of the ancient healing system of Ayurveda for thousands of years, and Ayurveda remains the oldest continuous system of medicine on the planet. As you may already know, Ayurveda is deeply intertwined with the yogic tradition.

It's interesting to look at the practice of alchemy as we begin to integrate aromatherapy into our practice. The alchemical philosophy states that all things—be them plant, mineral or human—are made of spirit. Alchemists work to dissolve the gross body of its impurities, while condensing the soul body, where all the healing properties of a particular substance were believed to exist. The same thing happens with aromatherapy and the distillation of a plant's essential oils. The essence of the plant is extracted to create a potent medicine from which we can all benefit.

> As yoga teachers, are we not alchemists of the body and mind? When we practice yoga, we often experience layers of stress, anxiety and sadness melt away. Held patterns of anger, pain and grief come boiling up to the surface to be dissolved. It's as if we are shedding our own impurities, becoming more and more of who we truly are—soul, spirit, unconditional love. As with the plant, we become human medicine. We become healers. When we work as human healers interfacing with the healers of the plant kingdom, a synergy takes place, and we can bring this beautiful combination of healing energy into our yoga classroom.

Each plant essence has a different healing effect. As such, we can actually theme entire yoga classes around a particular essential oil.

Let's take lavender essential oil.

Lavender essential oil balances the central nervous system and does so almost instantaneously. One idea would be to theme a yin or restorative class around lavender essential oil for calm and relaxation. Placing a few diffusers around the classroom and filling the air with soothing lavender mist as your students breathe and move will greatly enhance their experience. You may also want to cover their eyes with lavender-infused eye pillows during savasana.

Need a boost of energy before teaching a vinyasa class? Peppermint essential oil is an effective pick-me-up. For those high energy vinyasa classes or invigorating hatha sequences, you may want to diffuse peppermint and eucalyptus essential oils into the classroom.

An uplifting, *let's leave the winter doldrums behind* class would utilize the naturally anti-depressant effects of sweet orange oil. Each essential oil has its own mood. Theming your classes around them is one more creative way to add an extra special touch as you take your students through their yogic journey.

In your own personal practice you might mix your essential oil of choice with a carrier oil such as jojoba, olive, sweet almond or coconut oil. Rub the blend into your hands, then make a cup of your hands and inhale deeply for a few breaths. Then, rub the oil into your arms, neck and shoulders, and proceed with meditation or savasana.

These aromatherapy techniques bring about potent states of relaxation due to the nature in which essential oils work on our bodies, minds and spirits. When massaged into the skin they become a liquid medicine, calming the physical tissues with their anti-inflammatory properties. When inhaled, they calm our emotions because of the nose-brain connection.

Whenever we smell essential oils, their molecules go through the nose and up into our olfactory neurons (the nerve cells of the smelling system). The molecules then travel up to the olfactory bulb, which is right between the eyes. There's a track that goes directly to the brain, and the brain's nerve cells take the molecules directly into the brain.

We see here that the true organ of smell is, in fact, the brain. All of this happens in the most primitive, limbic part of the brain, sometimes referred to as the emotional brain. This is why, when we smell something, it triggers a thought or emotion instantaneously.

Some essential oils are even believed to open the heart center. Lavender, geranium, jasmine, neroli, rose, sandalwood and ylang ylang are all great examples. Many essential oil companies sell heart blends, which you can rub directly onto the heart chakra before meditation practice or savasana. Like Ayurveda, the healing art of aromatherapy works really well as a complement to your yoga practice.

Cultivate heart-centered awareness

One of the primary aims of yoga is to amplify and strengthen our awareness, as well as our identification with the heart, in order to be who we really are. The more we put our attention there, the stronger it gets. Our attention is one of the most powerful tools we have.

Choosing to live in tune with the divine intelligence of your heart is one of the most courageous choices you'll ever make. Following your heart will take you on a wild ride, but it will be the greatest adventure of your life—and that's what you as a yoga teacher get to experience. Then you get to share this newfound heartfelt awareness with your students, and everyone with whom you connect. By leading from the heart we create healthier relationships and healthier physiology. We even access a greater level of creativity and intuition.

Many yoga traditions recognize the heart as the seat of individual consciousness, and the center of life itself. In yoga, the heart is considered both literally and figuratively to be the guide or internal guru. Many practices teach us how to bring our awareness into the heart center.

The heart has been found to have its own independent nervous system—a complex system referred to as the brain inside the heart. There are at least forty thousand neurons in the heart, and the heart's intrinsic nervous system relays more information to the brain than the brain relays to the heart.

The heart feels not only every cell in the body, but also what happens outside of the body. It's truly the core of our human existence. Think of the phrase, *let's get to the heart of the matter.* It means, *let's get to the root, or the core.* It takes great courage to live from the heart - hence why the word *courage*, as well as *heart* and *core* all find their origins in the same Latin word, *cor.*

We all grapple with this universal human dilemma—finding balance between our heads and our hearts—especially in the West, where the winner is typically the most headstrong. Take a look around and you'll see a culture where many people live their lives from this mental headspace. If you ask someone where their awareness lies, they'll say, *in my head, of course*. While the mind is important and serves its purpose, there's a huge piece of the puzzle missing in our lives. The mental chatter of our minds limits our spiritual growth and development.

In 1969 I traveled to a refugee camp in the foothills of the Himalayas in India, where I witnessed a culture that lived from a heart-centered consciousness. It was like nothing I'd seen before. The female refugees of this special place displayed a vital energy and level of awareness so high I could hardly believe something like this was possible. The way they sang, the way they went about their daily lives—the whole place was nothing short of miraculous. Sadly, some years later I returned to find the citizens had integrated into modern society, losing the warm essence of heart-centered living in the process. But they had shown me that it was possible.

Heart-centered awareness is the answer to so many human problems. The heart will tell you when you *feel* love—not your brain. Fear and insecurity reside in the mind. They simply do not exist in the heart. Many of us find ourselves searching and longing for the abundance and freedom of the heart.

When you take a quiet moment to think about it, you may find that it's like two people have been living within you your entire life. There's the mind—a busy, demanding, and calculating aspect. Then there's the heart, whose still, small voice of wisdom you may hear once in a blue moon, or attend to on a special (or desperate) occasion.

As you listen to your heart more and more, and integrate its guidance into your life, your inner-voice—your innate wisdom of discernment—will begin to guide you. Your heart's discriminating awareness will awaken and strengthen. You'll start to distinguish between its guidance and the various clamorous and enthralling voices of your mind.

The memory of your true nature—with all its splendor and confidence and beauty—will return to you. You'll find that you've uncovered your own inner-guide. And this guide knows you through and through, increasing your clarity and humor, and helping you manage all the difficulties of your thoughts and emotions.

Your inner-guide is a joyful, tender, sometimes teasing presence who always knows what's best for you. It helps you navigate all the twists and turns of life's uncertainties, as you develop your relationship with it. Your guide will help you see the obsessive patterns of your habitual responses and confused emotions. As the voice of your heart grows stronger and clearer you will start to distinguish its truths from the various deceptions of the mind.

You will be able to listen to it with discernment and confidence. You may begin to see just how gripping and controlling the mind has been all these years, and you'll long for the space and freedom that comes with a life that's led by your heart. You may glimpse the exhilarating spaciousness of your true nature and you'll realize that for years, your mind—like a crazy con artist—has been swindling you with schemes, plans and promises.

Ultimately, the heart's all-revealing clarity and insight will show you distinctly and directly the beauty and subtlety of both your own inner and outer reality.

For me, yoga is primarily about moving from the head to the heart.

Practices for dropping our attention from our heads to our hearts

A truly effective yoga instructor teaches from a state of loving awareness. Certain ways of moving, breathing and being guide us to a place where we enter into a sphere of no-mind. We're not thinking about what's happening to our feelings or sensations and we find ourselves moving within a beautiful, uplifting field of energy. We're rooted in profound awareness and intuition. All of this happens when we learn to live from our hearts rather than our heads.

Energy flows where your attention goes.

Take your attention and direct it to your heart center. It's as easy as that. Our attention is so powerful. Water the seeds of love, and you'll get love. Give your heart the attention it needs to flourish, and soon your heartspace will naturally be your guide

Feel the heart as you speak.

Practice bringing your awareness to your heart as you speak. Imagine each word that leaves your mouth has its source in your heart center. You'd be surprised at the words that come out of your mouth. They're much more centered and grounded. If you've ever noticed people who talk from their heads—which is most of us—you can feel a sense of pervasive, restless energy. Upon moving to our heart and speaking from it, a calming, relaxing, and nurturing effect takes over.

When we live from the heart we are strengthening our intuition.

Tapping into the primal force of love that makes the world live and breathe enhances our lives in extraordinary ways. It also enhances the lives of all those we meet. This force lives in the heart center. Harness it, and you can move mountains.

The essence of intuitive yoga is to speak, move, feel, and lead from the heart. Bring your attention back to it, again and again. Just walk around, feeling your heart. Look at the trees. Feel your heart. Look at the floor. Feel your heart. Listen to the sounds of your surroundings. Feel your heart. Let your ears be a vehicle of the heart, so that your ears send messages to the heart first, instead of the brain. It may help to place a hand on the heart to bring your attention to it. Do this each time you practice dropping your awareness from head to heart.

When you look at a flower, don't think about the name of the flower, think about how beautiful it is. There's no need to say, *that's a harmonious hibiscus plant*. Instead, *feel* the plant. *Feel* its energy. Trust in all that is. *This* is intuitive yoga.

The yin & yang of movement

As you might have imagined, the yin and yang of movement originates from the teachings of the Chinese Yin Yang symbol, which represents balance. In yoga, movements can be considered either more yin or more yang. Depending upon what kind of effect we want for our students, we choose between these two opposite energies, which gracefully harmonize one another. The styles of yoga that grace most modern day gyms and yoga studios revolve around yang forms of movement. However, Yin Yoga, a fairly recent style, has become increasingly popular. Let's take a look at the different kinds of movements, so that we can best prepare classes to suit the many needs of our students.

Yang dynamic rhythmic & yang dynamic flowing

Yang movements generally build heat and strength in the body. There are two types of yang movements: dynamic rhythmic and dynamic flowing. Dynamic rhythmic movements are repetitive in nature, while dynamic flowing movements are fluid. The term "dynamic" refers to movement that is constantly changing. These styles of movement are most like traditional exercise.

To further illustrate the **yang dynamic rhythmic** style of yoga, think about taking any movement of the body—like lifting the knee towards the chest and placing it back down again—and repeating it rhythmically. In doing so, you create heat in the areas of the body that you're moving while increasing your heart rate and breath rate.

Over time the body grows stronger and more open, and the movement becomes more accessible. When we practice yang dynamic rhythmic movements we repetitively take our body to the edge, then back off, coming in and out of our full range of motion. As we do this again and again, the reflexes that signal the muscle to contract begin to relax and release. As this happens the movement becomes deeper and more fluid. Even gentle movements using resistance create the same effect.

Another example of yang dynamic rhythmic movement goes like this:

Place your feet apart in a warrior II stance. Once your feet are stable, inhale as you straighten your front leg. Exhale as you sink into warrior II. Continue this pattern. Notice the way your body responds as you repeat this dancing warrior for five to ten full breaths. Have you created heat in your front leg? See if you can sink even deeper into the pose each time you bend your front leg. Has your heart rate and breathing picked up? Be fully present with the sensations that arise.

Yang dynamic flowing styles of yoga are fluid in nature, such as the traditional sun salutations, as well as popular vinyasa flows. The effect can be intensely aerobic if you're moving at a substantial speed. It can also be more gentle and subtle, as you flow lightly and calmly through poses with the grace of a dancer. In each case the movements are fluid. They build heat and strength, relative to whatever tempo you choose to move through them.

While yang dynamic movement is not unlike traditional exercise, the key difference—which we spoke of before—is the consciousness you bring to it. When you head out for a jog you're moving your body in a rhythmic and repetitive way similar to yang dynamic yoga poses. In some cases, however, joggers aren't listening to their bodies as they move. They overstride, landing heel first with the foot ahead of the body's center of gravity, which increases the stress on the joints and, over time, injuries may follow.

We know that jogging is aerobically beneficial for our body, but when it has a traumatizing effect on the joints we need to change technique. If we can bring mindfulness to our exercise then jogging can be sustainable, but it takes a great deal of awareness. If you can come to a place in your jogging routine whereby there is little or no harm being done to the body then jogging can be yoga too—a yang, dynamic style. Imagine, yoga jogging! It's entirely possible with a heightened sense of consciousness to accompany each and every stride.

Yang dynamic movements can be affected by something called the *stretch reflex*. Almost every muscle in the body contains sensory receptors called muscle spindles. The muscle spindles inform the central nervous system (CNS) about changes in the length of our muscles and the speed of stretching. With this information we develop motor control, a steady posture, and a stable gait. The muscle spindles also regulate contraction of muscles by activating motor neurons via the stretch reflex. When there is a sudden change in the length of a muscle, the stretch reflex signals the muscle to contract in order to avoid injury.

Yang static movement

A yang static style of yoga maintains the yang aspect by producing heat and strength in the body while holding the pose, as opposed to moving dynamically. While yang dynamic movements can be affected by the stretch reflex—the contraction associated with a sudden lengthening of the muscle—the yang static approach can be affected by the *clasp-knife reflex*. The clasp-knife reflex is created by a type of sensory receptor found in the muscles tendons, called the Golgi Tendon Organ (GTO). The GTO senses changes in muscle tension and its function can be considered opposite of the muscle spindles. When there is a great deal of tension in the muscle, the GTO causes the muscle to relax by interrupting the contraction.

This takes us to a fascinating piece of yoga history. Yang static movements most closely resemble traditional yoga. When the great yogis came to the West with their vast treasure trove of yoga poses—which they held for what seemed like eons in Western time—the students were baffled. *Why would you hold a weird position like that? And for such a long time?* For them, the familiar yang dynamic style of movement made sense. However, the holding of the posture for thirty seconds or more, did not. These yogis knew something the rest of us didn't.

As you come into an asana that lengthens a particular muscle, the muscle spindle causes the muscle to contract to protect it from tearing. The initial tightness you feel any time you begin to stretch a muscle, reflects this inner process. The sensation is noticeably felt.

When most people exercise, they don't understand that if they wait a sensation out, the contraction caused by the muscle spindle will eventually be interrupted by the GTO, which causes the muscle to relax. Coincidentally, it takes about thirty seconds for relaxation to occur. This was the minimum amount of time the old-time-yogis held their asana. They knew that after the initial thirty seconds, they could move even deeper into the pose. This is the essence of yang static yoga movements. It's a fascinating phenomenon, and I encourage you to get familiar with it. It applies to every muscle in the body, and is one of the main reasons yoga feels so good.

This concept is yet another example of the connection between Western science and ancient yogic principles and techniques. The clasp-knife reflex which releases muscle tension is just another way of expressing what the ancient yogis intuited thousands of years ago.

The next time an exercise enthusiast says, *I don't get yoga. They hold poses for so long. How does it all work?* You can respond with, *Oh, that's a yang static practice—one of four methods of yogic movement. It works by using the clasp-knife reflex, and has wonderful benefits for the body.*

You could also talk about a jogger with tight hamstrings. Yang static movement would be great for them. They would benefit from a forward fold held for a full thirty seconds, or five to six deep breaths. During the forward fold the GTO will employ the clasp-knife reflex, thereby releasing tension, compression, and contraction. And it will happen with greater efficacy than if the pose was held for only five to ten seconds.

Yin static movement, or Yin Yoga

Yin static movement is the last type of Hatha yoga we'll explore. As we've touched upon earlier, the term *static* refers to a pose that's held for a long period of time. Yin yoga, also referred to as Taoist yoga—is all about the health of the connective tissue in the body. You can think of it as yoga for the joints and connective tissues, as opposed to the muscles.

Yin yoga also finds roots in ancient yoga traditions when yogis instructed their students to hold poses for a long period of time. Two to five minutes is a typical time frame to hold a yin yoga pose today.

Let's explore the style in detail, so that we can better understand the *how* and *why* of its inner workings.

As with yang static movement, traditional exercise enthusiasts have voiced a bit of confusion and skepticism around the efficacy of yin static poses, causing intriguing debates among exercise and yoga communities. Again, the scientific evidence that supports yin yoga is all about the extended time period in which poses are held.

It's important to remember that the connective tissues around joints are thick and strong—especially those enveloping the hip region. While traditional exercise fails to address the fact that these tissues can be compressed and lengthened in order to reduce and relieve joint stress, yin static movement does just that.

It takes anywhere from two to five minutes for the fibers of the connective tissues in a joint to relax and lengthen. During the first two minutes, the body tries to maintain the integrity of the pose by using muscular effort. After a certain period of time, and after the muscles relax, the connective tissues begin to open. When this opening occurs, hydration is stimulated within the joint capsule, bringing about rejuvenation and regeneration.

While yin yoga doesn't challenge the muscles like dynamic forms of yoga do, it *does* challenge the mind—encouraging it to let go and relax—a great challenge for us modern day yoga practitioners. The health benefits of yin static movements are vast, and the effect on the body's larger joints can relieve back pain, improve posture, and increase joint health.

The thing is, joints need exercise just as much as muscles do, and on an energetic level—even more so. When we bring movement into a joint capsule we increase the circulation of synovial fluid in the joint. It's like putting oil on a rusty hinge. When this happens, hyaluronic acid in the joint increases.

Yin yoga isn't just about the body, it's also a profound practice in mindfulness. When we move slowly into a pose, paying attention to every detail of bodily sensation, we understand where our edge is. We breathe into this place to create deep openings. This brings about tremendous physical and energetic changes in the body *and* mind.

Ligaments surround every joint capsule. They're some of the strongest connective tissues in the body. Many people think of ligaments as being rigid, like bones. But, they're not. When you sprain your ankle, the ligaments on one side of the ankle joint lengthen dramatically, which creates an unstable joint. But ligaments can be lengthened in a balanced way without causing injury or pain, and that's what we aim to do in yin yoga. Ligaments are like leather belts which you can stretch over time—you should not pull them too hard or too fast—but giving them constant tension over time releases and lengthens them. Ligaments need this constant pressure for two to five minutes during a pose.

When you create an opening in a joint capsule, synovial fluid is released. Synovial fluid is the lubrication that protects the joint. Without movement, the joints stiffen and dry up, becoming less and less mobile.

Yin yoga is founded upon ligament and tendon health. It's a principle that almost every other form of exercise overlooks. This makes a yin yoga practice an important tool in your yogi toolbox. And as you teach yin yoga poses you'll want to give this information to your students to further motivate them, and entice them to keep coming back to class.

Yin static movement is closely linked to the theory of prana/chi we looked at earlier. Yin yoga pioneer Paul Grilley believes the energetic pathways of nadis/meridians may have a physical component found in the network of hyaluronic acid that exists throughout the body, and especially in the joints.

Hyaluronic acid is a substance which binds hundreds of times its weight in water. It plays an important role in wound regeneration. In joints it is generated within the synovial fluid that surrounds them. Through attentive movement like yoga we increase the amount of synovial fluid in the joint, which increases the amount of hyaluronic acid, and then—according to Grilley's theory—more life force energy. In the same way a vein or artery moves blood through the body, hyaluronic acid collects water molecules and energy moves along the meridian pathways. Instead of pumping blood through the heart, we're pumping energy throughout the body by way of movement.

On a physical level yin yoga is the perfect practice to prepare us for sitting meditation. It's a discipline that more and more yogis are realizing is essential for their mental, emotional, and spiritual wellbeing. When we sit in meditation we're aiming for a long spine that's supported by the vertical alignment of the pelvis. Yin poses encourage and support this alignment.

It's true that ashtanga, kundalini, vinyasa, and other dynamic yoga styles help us prepare to sit and meditate. However, the passive yin style is also a great complement to our meditation practice. While the yang styles of movement focus on the muscles, yin yoga targets the deep connective tissues of the body—tendons, ligaments and fascia. As we sit in meditation, with a long spine and open hips, we rely upon the flexibility of our connective tissues to support us. A gentle stretch which we hold for a longer period of time makes connective tissues grow longer and stronger.

Another very cool aspect of a yin yoga practice is this:

It builds self-awareness.

As with anything in life, the slower we go, the more present we must be. It's much easier to gloss over our issues when flowing through a vigorous ashtanga sequence, or dance-like vinyasa practice. But when we slow down and become rooted in the here and now, stuff just naturally bubbles up. This is something we want to let happen. We want to support it. A yin practice does just this.

Which leads us to the Ayurvedic concept of *ama*.

Ama is anything that remains undigested within our bodies. This could be undigested food that produces mucus and leaves us heavy and lethargic. It could be thoughts and emotions that were never processed, leaving us depleted and depressed and building up in our emotional bodies. Ama could even be words left unsaid.

You may have heard that old emotions, or emotional ama, are stored in the hips. You may have even experienced a release of sadness, fear, frustration, anxiety or anger in a hip opening yoga class. When we mindfully bring our bodies into a hip-opening pose and hold that pose for a long period of time we release accumulated ama.

The hips are one of the largest storehouses of old emotions. In the sequence that follows, we'll take a look at some of the best yin poses to do each morning to rid the body of stuck emotions.

When we teach (and practice) yin yoga it's important to reiterate this:

Muscles need to be relaxed in order for their underlying tissues to do all the stretching and strengthening that needs to be done.

The library of yin yoga poses is smaller than the library of hatha yoga poses for this very reason. Arm balances, standing postures, inversions—these poses require the action of the muscles. Yin postures don't. We also execute yin poses in a different way than we do yang postures. In yin we focus on releasing the muscle rather than contracting it. This is one reason the names of yin poses differ from their yang counterparts.

In essence, they're different poses.

Mini yin practice: shoelace pose—swan pose—savasana—meditation

This is an ideal sequence for cleansing ama from the hips, and promoting spinal health.

1. To begin, bring yourself to sit in a cross-legged position.
2. Place your right leg beneath your left, wiggling a bit to move your knees on top of one another. If this isn't comfortable for your bottom leg, straighten that leg out, into what we call *half-shoelace*.

Don't worry about this being a lesser posture. Think of it as a *different* posture—one that works different parts of the body. What you're looking for is a position that's a little bit juicy for your hips. If you're doing full shoelace you may want to sit on a block.

3. Next, we twist. Gently hold onto the top knee with the opposite hand and bring the other hand behind you. From your torso, twist to the left. Breathe here for several breaths. Then return to center and fold forward ever so slightly, until you come to the goldilocks position—not too much and not too little. Remember to keep your muscles relaxed so that the connective tissues underneath can stretch and strengthen.
4. Rest your chest or forehead on a bolster if you have one. Or rest your elbows on a block. Snuggle back into the hips so that the hips stay grounded on the earth. Stay here for five minutes or longer.

From here we transition into The Swan.

5. Bring the top leg all the way back behind you—as you would for pigeon pose. You might want to bring the front knee underneath you so that you're sitting on your heel, while walking the hands backwards to come into a slight backbend. Breathe here for a few minutes.
6. Come deeper into swan by taking your foot out from beneath you and forward, flexing that front foot. The right sit bone is on the floor, or supported with a cushion or a block.
7. Slowly and gently walk your hands forward into sleeping swan and snuggle back into the hips. Walk the hands a little further and snuggle back into the hips some more. Come onto your forearms or rest them on a bolster. Breathe into your hips and relax into the sensations that you feel. Close your eyes and visualize your hips opening. Use your exhalations to soften and relax. Stay here for several breaths.

From here, transition into downward facing dog. Stay here for 3-5 cycles of breath. As you breathe, move the body in whatever way feels good. You may want to pedal out your feet as you feel the opening in your calf muscles. Maybe sway the hips from side to side. As you move, take some time to drop in and savor the sensations. They should feel good.

Shoelace, second side

1. From downward facing dog, come down to your knees.
2. Move your body into shoelace pose on the other side, this time with the left leg beneath the right. Again, do the twist and hold for several breaths.
3. Come back to center and move forward ever so slowly. When you come to your edge be very still and breathe. Unprocessed emotions may float to the surface. If you feel the need to cry, cry. Let the *issues in your tissues* come up and out. Simply be with your thoughts, your emotions, and the physical sensations of the body. Practice presence.

Downward facing dog to savasana

1. Again, move into downward facing dog, and really bring your awareness to the body. Feel the sensations that arise, and savor them as your body opens further.
2. Come to a kneeling position and then to your back, preparing for savasana. Relax in savasana for several minutes.
3. Roll to your side and pause for a few breaths. Push up to a cross-legged sitting position and notice the openness in your hips. Sit in meditation for as long as you like.

If you're new to yin yoga, give it a chance. Practice this sequence every day for a week to let the practice sink in. Enjoy its life-giving effects.

Let's review

We've just explored four primary types of yogic movement—yang dynamic rhythmic, yang dynamic flowing, yang static, and yin static. All forms create heat, length, and life force in the most important regions of the body, such as the hips and spine. Once mobility is established in the hips and spine we then direct our attention to the extremities, as well as the smaller joints of the body.

This is essentially the foundation of all yoga classes. *Intuitive yoga* adheres to all of these principles while teaching students how to diagnose their own sensations.

Now think of your most favorite style of yoga. Is it Hatha? Ashtanga? Anusara? Vinyasa? Kundalini? Iyengar? Does your favorite form of yoga include yang dynamic rhythmic movement, yang dynamic flowing movement, yang static movement, or yin static movement?

Do you know what makes Bikram yoga so wildly popular? It's not just the heat.

Many styles of yoga take place in heated rooms. Bikram is appealing to Westerners because it works primarily with the yang static form of movement. In the Bikram series, students are taught to hold a pose until they feel an energetic release—the life force energy that comes from holding a pose steadily and for a substantial amount of time. Bikram yoga is simply an adaptation from a traditional form of yoga to a modern one.

On the flip side, Bikram Yoga is not healthy for each and every *body.* For students who like the demanding psychological and physical efforts necessary to take a Bikram class, the style is great. And while hot yoga projects an elitist attitude at times, it's important to let that notion go as you teach your students the importance of choosing a yoga class that feels right for *them.*

Just because a yoga class takes place in a hot room it does not make it better, harder, or more beneficial for every yoga practitioner. We all have different constitutions, which means we're all going to differ in the styles we choose to practice *and* teach.

During 200-hour yoga teacher training at Yandara we explore the pros and cons of many styles of yoga. We note the different feelings invoked by each style, which helps us better understand our bodies and ourselves. In doing so we discover which styles of yoga we might want to teach and which ones are best left to our peers.

An Anusara class tends to leave students with a feeling that's entirely different from a Bikram one. Yin yoga brings forth sensations that feel quite unlike those of a vinyasa style class. We explore how these yoga styles fit together, the history of their movement, and the personality of the teachers who created these different brands of yoga. They all have different psychological effects on each student, which keeps things interesting for us—not only as teachers, but also as lifelong students of yoga!

Every style and each teacher plays an important role in making the yoga world the diverse community it is today. Regardless of what style of yoga you teach, and what form of movement you choose as your mode of expression, it's necessary to understand some basic anatomical concepts when teaching a class that generates life force energy within the body.

Guidelines for breathwork

When it comes to pranayama we want to keep it as simple as possible. While there are many ancient pranayama techniques designed to move prana through the body using conscious breath control, knowledge of all of these practices isn't necessary to teach effective yoga classes.

Your typical yoga student doesn't need an in-depth pranayama practice. Pranayama is a powerful yogic art and, as such, it should be instructed by a teacher with expert training in this particular discipline. For our intents and purposes simplicity is best while working with the breath, and we can do a world of good by teaching simple yet conscious breathing techniques.

Most of us breathe shallow breaths in a sympathetic pattern. This means that we typically breathe from a place high in the chest, with rapid cycles of inhalation and exhalation. It's the same pattern used by animals in the survival mode of fight or flight. In other words, most people breathe in a way that perpetuates stress—and we want to teach how to breathe in a way that relaxes and soothes the nervous system and activates the parasympathetic system. One way of doing this is through deep belly breathing.

Did you know that babies breathe from their bellies?

Belly breathing is the way humans are meant to breathe when we are relaxed—with long inhales drawn in toward the belly and smooth exhales out from the belly area. This type of breathing allows prana to flow freely through the body while moving through yoga poses. It's the foundational technique that all yoga teachers should be aware of.

Prana inside and out

In addition to the intrinsic life force within each and every one of us, there's also an external one. We'll call this our energetic field. One of the goals of yoga is to strengthen this field of energy.

Our energetic field radiates outward to about three or four feet beyond the body in all directions. Energetic practices such as yoga, tai chi, and chi gong strengthen this field of energy. When we increase the amount of life force energy moving through our bodies, we also extend it out beyond our body to radiate peace and purity.

In the same way acupuncture works to release areas in the body where there's blocked energy flow, yoga breaks up these blockages to create a smooth river of life throughout the entire body. As we gradually release and let go of these energy blocks the external energy field also strengthens and expands.

To illustrate the concept of prana even further, imagine that you're a light bulb.

Life force energy flows through your core like the flow of energy through the filament of a light bulb. In you *and* the light bulb energy wants to radiate out from this core. In a light bulb energy can't radiate as light unless it's surrounded by a glass bulb.

Imagine the physical edges of your body are the thin glass that surrounds the filament of a light bulb. The glass *and* the body contain the source of light *and* the means of radiating that light outward.

Without the glass bulb the filament can't radiate out to its fullest potential. Without your physical form *you* can't express the pure light that lives within.

This illustrates the perfect balance between containment and expansion, and it's what true energetic practice is all about.

Now imagine your body as a light bulb that draws its energy from the core of the earth. With your feet rooted to the core of the earth draw life force energy into yourself. Through the container of your physical skin you radiate this life force out into the world. Consider how your movement practice might change if you were to move with this image in your mind.

I once had a tai chi teacher who helped me look deeply into this concept—that of containing and radiating energy throughout the physical body. Together we studied yoga classes to observe the way students were using, losing, or generating energy. All it took to see this was a willing heart and open eyes. I saw students who had no idea how to use their bodies as a container for energy. Energy kept leaking out. They actually looked tired as they practiced.

How could I teach people to move without this loss of energy?

This thought kept coming to me.

I discovered this:

It's not the *way* of moving that needs to change, it's the *consciousness* around it.

In fact, there's no external effort or change required—only attention to the practice of being the light bulb, so to speak.

Remind your students to be present to the energetic sensations of the body. Continually bring them from their heads to their bodies as you guide them through the poses. While the shift in attention is inherently simple and subtle, the movement experience changes dramatically. This way of practicing allows us to gain strength without exhausting our stores of energy. In fact, you actually feel rejuvenated afterwards.

While these teachings are ancient, they're also quite natural. With an energetic practice, however, the physical changes in the body are subtle, which can be challenging. The subtlety makes it difficult for us to realize the sheer importance of this energetic practice in our daily lives. But the more we do it the more sensitive we become. Which makes it much easier to pinpoint what's happening.

Imagine your energy practice is like planting a seed in your consciousness. This seed is a new way of being and will take time to grow. To nurture the seed into maturity, love and attention is needed each day. Celebrate the tiny shifts in your feelings and behaviors. These are the fruits of your energy practice. And pay attention when your behavior changes for the better. It will.

For example, you might say no to a sugary treat and yes to a snack that deeply nourishes your body. Maybe you let go of an unhealthy habit or respond with patience to a negative situation. Remind your students (and yourself) that these subtle shifts might take weeks, months, or even years to see. And yet, even as you read these words, they're positively affecting who you are. Your consciousness is taking them in, and eventually you'll see that small changes blossom in your external experience.

Yandara morning flow

One of the first ideas we developed at the Yandara Yoga Institute is intended to get students out of their habitual thought patterns. It's a movement sequence called *the morning flow.* This morning flow is designed around my beliefs as to what yoga is and why it works. It targets all the major parts of the body—starting with the spine, and then moving into the larger hip and shoulder joints—and out to the smaller joints and extremities.

The idea behind this flow focuses on the way the poses flow together to create a specific kind of energy. The movements in and of themselves are nothing revolutionary—and yet it ignites a feeling of grace and demands a gentle attentiveness to the self in order to stay balanced.

The Yandara morning flow is a soothing dance with yourself that, when done slowly and with conscious attention to the subtle sensations that arise, can have profound effects on the body.

In addition, the morning flow demonstrates the differences between the four types of yogic movement previously described. I typically teach the morning flow in the yang dynamic style and the yang static style. First we build heat, moving with the breath in a yang dynamic flowing fashion. Then we repeat the same sequence. This time, however, we hold each pose for five to six breaths, demonstrating the other type of release that occurs when practicing yang dynamic static movement.

There's also a floor series in the morning flow that can be done in either yang dynamic flowing, yang dynamic static, or yin static style, depending upon the effect you want the practice to have on yourself or your student. Through this repetitive sequence, and by utilizing each style of movement, I find that students get really familiar with what the sweet spot is for them in each pose. They also get used to which parts of their body are being affected by each movement and learn to adjust the style of movement in order to find that sweet spot throughout the practice.

In the morning flow, it's never about doing it *right*, it's about feeling *good*.

There's also an emphasis on not overdoing it, which can be difficult for teacher trainees to get used to. So many of us have the *more is better* belief ingrained in our minds. This is yet another reason why the morning flow is essential. In creating a sequence that demands slow, attentive movement within a safe range of motion, students are able to sense what it feels like when the body says, *enough is enough*.

It's at this point when the body contracts to protect itself. Through practice and awareness, we can sensitize ourselves to that contraction, learning to honor our body when it speaks up. Connecting to these points of contraction moves us beyond our conditioned stopping points. We naturally soften into deeper expressions and more genuine explorations of what our body is capable of.

The Yandara flow sequence not only targets all major parts of the body, it's also adjustable and easy to do anytime and anywhere. Over the years I've introduced a few nontraditional yoga poses to enhance this unique aspect of it. One of them is surfer pose. Another is surrender pose, which is at the heart of the sequence.

The sequence is designed to be done slowly and to create a gracefulness of movement in the body. As you practice it over and over you can take this intrinsic sense of ease and grace and apply it to any style of yoga—hatha, Ashtanga, vinyasa, and so on. Grace and mindfulness go hand-in-hand, and this is an element that will enhance your teaching for the longevity of your yoga teaching career.

In fact, this quality of centeredness and grace is one you'll want to practice your entire life. As you become a more experienced teacher you'll find that doing poses quickly or rapidly, or using jerky or jarring movements is counterintuitive in nature. You'll desire centeredness, and while your movements don't always have to be gentle or slow, they'll need to exude a vital awareness that comes from a very centered place within.

An intuitive morning flow class

Let's lay out a typical morning flow sequence—as taught to our teacher trainees.

The actual sequences are important, but also important is the general framework for moving people into this desired state of being—the one where we drop our conditioned habits and behaviors. I've also made notes of *things to consider* for each part of the class. These are topics I bring up, or comments I make to deepen the experiences throughout our practice. Teacher trainees typically leave wanting a record of how these morning flows take place. This is my way of answering their request.

Warm-up

There are so many ways to warm up the body. You'll want to choose a method that feels good in your body on a given day. Then, trust this will also be the one that feels best for your students.

Dance dance dance!

Any way you like! Shake your arms, legs, and hips. Hop around. Explore the space of your mat. Turn up the music. Get moving. Your students will usually tire of this warm-up after a minute or so. It's at this point when I like to remind them that if I took them to a bar on a Friday night, they'd most likely dance for hours on end.

Shake your body

Note: It's my policy that as a teacher you must make a fool of yourself as early in the class as possible. This gets the worry of that happening out of the way. Shaking the body is an ideal way to make a fool of yourself and bring some humor and lightness to the class!

Scrunch and relax the face a few times. Now shake your hands in different directions and in different ways than you're used to. Turn your palms out. Turn your palms in. Shake the forearms. Now tighten the forearms so you isolate the upper arms without shaking the elbow joint. Tighten your fist, isolating your biceps and triceps. Let that go. Now shift your weight to the right foot. Shake your left foot (be careful with your knee joint as you shake). Tighten the calf muscles. Curl the toes up and isolate the upper thighs. Feel yourself centered and balanced. Release the right foot. Shake! Engage the calf muscles. Shake the upper leg.

Allow your attention to be in the present moment—on your abdominal area, thighs, and buttocks. Release tension in the upper part of the body. Relax the shoulders and roll the neck from side to side. But don't shake the head—it's a little bit dangerous—simply move it from side to side as you scrunch up the face a bit. You might feel a little tension—that's not a bad thing. We're just looking for as many ways as we can to create relaxation rather than caution.

Now come back to neutral. Step your feet apart and begin with abdominal lifts. Now shake the internal organs. Shake the exterior part of the body. Open the pelvis by rocking it back and forth. Inhale. Exhale and hold it out while gyrating the belly button in and out. Activate the abdominal muscles. Keep breathing so you don't get lightheaded. Now feel the energy you've created. This is a very effective warm up.

Jog on the spot

Jog mindfully in place. Pay attention to what areas of the body need more support. Adjust your movement so that it feels good. In this warm-up you can retrain your students to run in a way that's both healthy and mindful.

Self-massage

Start by gently massaging the body to warm it up. Create a slow, beautiful kind of moving meditation as you massage. You can gently sway the body from side to side as you massage your feet, your ankles, and calves. You may want to do a body scan to feel what areas need attention. Massage the body from head to toe, or toe to head. Take your healing hands and rub with the intention of warming, lengthening, and loosening your entire body.

Mindful massage is an excellent way to prepare the body for movement.

Note: It can be interesting to warm one side of the body through movement and the other side through massage, and then to compare the two.

Warm-ups are a great time to flex our creativity muscles. Any movements during the warm-up period are fine, as long they build heat in the body—especially in the spine and abdomen. There's really no right or wrong way to lead a warm-up. Music is a nice addition because it really brings people into the present moment. Alternatively, you could spend time during the warm-up to create a sacred space. This will probably feel strange to beginners—but with time, everyone embraces this ritual. It's a way of reminding your students that this isn't a space connected to home, work, or wherever they've just been.

This is where you set the tone for your students—a tone that requires a greater level of attention. Opening with the sound of OM, a chant that rings true for you, or a reading from a spiritual text will create an environment that brings people out of their habitual thought patterns. If you're going to set a theme or intention for a class, this is the time to do so. If you do, be sure to reinforce it intermittently throughout the class.

Optional warm-up exercises

It's always nice to change up the flow of movement by adding something new to your classes. The warm-up is an ideal time to do this—it's the time when your students move from their heads and into their bodies, and when they're more open to new experiences and not yet fatigued. Introduce eye asanas, tai chi movements, a qigong sequence, or creative forms of the sun salutations.

Yandara standing series

This is where we begin the more traditional movement portion of the class. This particular sequence is listed in the appendix. During the standing portion of class you can use any sequence of movement you like. Make you check in with your students often, and consider asking the following questions from time to time:

- What are you feeling in this particular moment? Is it too much in any way? Is your body asking you to back off?
- Can you feel the rootedness of your feet? See if you can draw the source of your energy up from the center of the earth.
- What would happen right now if you weren't thinking?
- There is a certain aliveness within you. How can you tap into this essence and grace?
- Imagine you're a brilliant dancer moving from your most beautiful and inspired place. This is the truest expression of your soul in this moment. This is your body moving with profound ease and grace.

After you've done the sequence, and slowly warmed up into it—dynamically moving in and out of poses—you move into the yang static portion of the flow. This is where you hold poses for three to five breaths, and when you really begin to feel into the sensations of the pose. It's here where you understand the elements of tension, compression and proportion within the body. These longer holds help us gain present moment awareness within the pose, to better discern what's happening.

As you take in energy from the earth to ground you you're truly aware of what pose you're in. Unlike yang dynamic movement, yang static movement allows you to get deeply grounded and aware that you're in, say, warrior II, or transitioning out of warrior III.

Mindfulness of movement comes more naturally because you have time to drop into the actual pose and practice being mindful.

Always remember this:

You might come into a pose and it may be too much. But once you've learned how to diagnose your sensations you'll know when you've gone too far. It might even be painful. You're not necessarily going to physically hurt yourself. It won't even be damaging to you within the grander scheme of things—but what happens is, every time you assume a posture that's too much—one that's causing pain that you're contracting around—your body remembers.

Then, it will associate that particular posture with pain. The next time your body meets the posture it will work to protect you even more than before. The body becomes stressed and tightens up. This is what we want to avoid. And while your mind might notice the tensing, it will likely tell you to push on. And if you do there's a bit of physical and psychological damage that occurs. This is why we always work to find the Goldilocks position—not too much and not too little. We're extremely careful around our edge. If there's not enough challenge the mind will wander. If there's too much the body contracts, protects and stores the tension of the posture in its somatic memory.

Floor series

In the floor series it's a good idea to incorporate abdominal work. Core movements support circulatory, digestive, and emotional health and well-being. You can also create your own ways of inviting sensation into these regions of the body.

Whatever sequence you choose, try to check in with what your students are feeling as you move. I like to ask students to consider the following when flowing through the floor series:

- Feel the heat that you've created through your movement. How can you use this energy to release this part of your body?
- When you find your edge—the point where your body says, *that's enough*—see what happens when you hang out there for a minute or two.
- Find a sensation in your body that can hold your attention without being alarming.
- What are you enjoying in *this* particular moment? Enjoyment is one of my favorite themes for a yoga class.

Savasana

Savasana is a very important part of a class. No matter what happens in the movement part of your class, as long as you give your students a good, long savasana, they'll leave feeling rested and rejuvenated.

Sometimes, I like to sing to my students as they lie in savasana. This is yet another way to work with your own feelings of vulnerability and to inspire students to move through their own moments of uncertainty with compassion. A reading or song that moves you is a nice way of bringing your personal touch to savasana.

Most importantly, I ask them to take a moment to feel whether or not the body is still hanging on to stress, and to let it go if necessary. As a general rule, ten percent of your yoga class should be spent in savasana. That means, if you teach a sixty minute class, be sure to give your students at least a six minute savasana.

When a teacher loses track of time in class it's typically savasana that's cut short. Don't let that happen in your class. Students are always thankful for savasana as a precious time for relaxation and restoration.

As we work through these concepts keep in mind that your primary intention as an intuitive yoga teacher is to move your students into their hearts. Throughout this book we'll continually return to the heart—opening our awareness to ways of dropping into our hearts, moment by moment.

One of the best ways to do this is through the breath. Our breath automatically draws us into our heart centers. In fact, the element of air is closely associated with the heart chakra. Every time we practice pranayama we come out of our heads and into our hearts. When we focus our attention on our heartspace, relaxation naturally follows.

When you ask your students to breathe in, remind them that their inhalations are creating space in the cavity around the heart. On the exhalation, give them permission to breathe out fear, moving into the expanding heartspace created by the breath.

Anatomy for the intuitive yoga teacher

As an intuitive yoga teacher, it's essential to understand some basic anatomical concepts in order to give your students the profound benefits of a life force generating yoga class. This is the case regardless of what movement type you choose as your mode of expression. You won't need to know everything about anatomy or be some kind of physical therapist to teach yoga. Basic anatomical concepts are all you need to keep your students safe while confidently clarifying yoga postures and yogic movement.

The anatomical concepts most essential for our intents and purposes are: compression, tension, and proportion. For a more in-depth discussion of these concepts, and with visual support, I encourage you to watch Paul Grilley's DVD, *The Anatomy of Yoga*—a resource I utilize in my yoga teacher trainings.

Within every yoga pose there are certain limitations, and though these limitations don't exist for everyone there are certain poses you'll find that, as a teacher, some of your students will simply be unable to do. Understanding why exactly a person can't place their body in a particular position is linked to your understanding of these concepts: compression, tension and proportion.

Without an understanding of these terms, yoga teachers might as well recite a fixed set of cues to orient people's bodies into a certain position—without any consideration of the fact that some bodies may not be built to move into these postures. This is not the approach that we as intuitive yoga teachers want to take.

So how do the terms tension and compression apply to our yoga practice? The common explanation is that tension is a force brought about by pulling or lengthening an object, while compression is a force created by pushing or shortening the amount of space or length an object has.

In a bodily sense, compression happens with any bone to bone joint limitation. An example of this would be in the elbow. Straighten your arm out in front of you. Then, from the elbow, straighten it as much as you can. Now imagine that I came along and tried to bend your elbow back even further—it's simply not going to happen, right? Because I'd be compressing your elbow joint and pushing one bone into another, where there's no anatomical room for give. A healthy elbow joint moves to the point of straightening and no further. With tension, on the other hand, when we stretch in a conscious manner, allowing the body to release tension, the body will become more flexible over time.

Teaching the art of body sensing

One of the most crucial elements in teaching your students the art and science of yoga is raising their awareness as to what their bodily sensations are telling them. The following exercise is one of the most powerful ways to do simply because of the fact that our legs are really strong. You won't hurt anyone through the repetition of this exercise, and it's a great way to tap into the sensations of pain and contraction.

Stand with your feet hip width apart, knees slightly bent. Swing the arms back and forth while releasing tension in the shoulders. You're naturally working your core muscles ever-so-slightly as you swing your arms. The legs also get a good workout. While this exercise might seem a little weird at first, it's beneficial to the body in a surprisingly powerful way.

As you guide your students through the exercise, bring their attention into the present moment. In the present moment, there's typically not much stress involved. Stress generally happens in our minds as we think back to the past or fantasize about the future. You might want to guide your students' attention to their breath as they move through this exercise because the breath is always anchored in presence.

As you do this, feel your legs and bend your knees slightly. Bending your knee joint is important. If you curl your toes a bit you'll engage the core. Now practice focusing on a fixed point somewhere in your environment—this is a steady gaze known as drishti in Sanskrit. As you do this see if you can *feel* your consciousness. Feel everything simultaneously—all the sensations. Try not to let the mind wander away from the practice. A wandering mind causes contraction in the body.

Let's explore the spine. First off, shift your weight to your right. Now, shift your weight to the left. Come into your center. Feel the consciousness in your body. Open and close the pelvic crease (also known as opening and closing the kua). This is one of the fundamental ways to get prana flowing through the nadis. Opening and closing the pelvic crease brings awareness to this part of the body. It brings energy to your root center. As you do this, relax the abdominal and shoulder muscles.

You'll feel like you're being fully held by the crown of your head. Come to the center. Flex and extend the spine. Really feel the opening in the pelvic area. Experiment by opening the spine in both directions. See how your breath just naturally works with your body? You don't have to *think* about your breathing. Your breathing automatically follows the openness of the body. Experience this enjoyment. It feels good. Let your heart experience the enjoyment.

Make sure your hips stay square, because you don't want to torque the knees. Every position of the body has a perfect way of being and working for you. Flex and extend the upper spine. Twist the upper spine. Find fluidity and peace.

Finding the zone

As yoga teachers we should learn how to be deeply present in our own bodies as we teach. This will translate to our students and they'll pick up on our presence, which will make them want to return to class again and again. The energy we create through our presence is inspiring. It makes our students want to be present too, enhancing everyone's experience in the process.

This is why we need our own sadhana. We need a personal yoga *and* meditation practice. We need to practice what we teach, so to speak. Every one of us has the wisdom and confidence to teach amazing yoga classes. Sometimes, it just takes getting out of our own way. Taking baby steps every day in the direction of this un-doing will help us create classes that truly inspire our students. This is much more important than knowing how to do a perfect downward facing dog or having the athletic ability to do a handstand.

Even beginning yoga teachers have access to an amazing field of information—one that enables them to teach incredibly inspiring yoga classes. You actually hold technical information stored from the many yoga classes you've taken throughout the years. This field of information is accessible because it's stored within your field of consciousness, even if it hasn't yet been stored in the memory of the brain.

When you teach (or practice teach) choose from the practices below to help you access this field of information. Remember—when the student has access to their heart consciousness and its basic fearlessness—creativity *and* practical information flow freely.

- We can access fear as a sensation, and we can use this sensation of fear to drop into our hearts. If you pay attention you'll find the sensation of fear is often located in the heart center.

- During teacher training, we find our gifts and talents as a teacher when we lead our peers through classes. Most of the time our peers see our intrinsic strengths and gifts better than we do. Therefore we encourage all students to express how they make each other feel during the practice teaching sessions, discovering each aspiring teacher's unique gift. This is a simple yet powerful practice.

- When you find out the effect your teaching has on another person your sense of self-worth is increased, which leads to less fear in teaching.

- Just as there are certain ideas and circumstances that shake up our teaching fears, there are ways to release these fears. We can do so by memorizing a particular yoga sequence that we love and teaching it often. We can turn to the natural repetition of our daily practice. We can memorize simple cueing and sequences. Repetition and memorization builds our field of confidence. So learning and practicing a simple set of sequences—as well as a simple set of cues—is incredibly helpful.

- Then there's the practice of simply describing what our bodies are doing as we teach and move through poses, instead of memorizing cues.

For example:

I'm inhaling while raising my arms up and stepping my left foot back.

(Dropping the *I* and *my* supports embodiment and presence as we teach.)

Inhale, raise the arms up, and step the left foot back.

Sometimes it works better to put the noun first:

Inhale, arms raise up, left foot steps back.

- As a practice teaching method some students prefer to imagine themselves not even teaching a class. In their minds they're simply describing out loud what they're doing as they move. This eases stress and brings them into the present moment.

- We sometimes ease our stress by being overly authoritative. This way of teaching can create separation. This might backfire, bringing about fearful sensations in both student and teacher.

- When we feel as if we're simply part of a beautiful group of people practicing postures together, balance of the inner and outer teacher springs forth.

- For some, not doing the postures while cueing is helpful.

- When teaching, imagine how good it would feel if the goal was to simply enjoy yourself. Pure and simple enjoyment in the moment—while recognizing what a beautiful thing it is to share our yoga practice with others—helps us teach with fearlessness.

  (When we see a teacher enjoying themselves we have permission to enjoy *ourselves*. It's very hard to feel joyful and fearful at the same time.)

- The yoga teacher trainer observes each student and then intuitively figures out the way that each student can access their gifts—usually by finding ways to encourage them to let go of stress and fear and let their true selves come through.

- For some of us, meditation is our primary practice. It helps us let go of the unnecessary baggage of fear that no longer serves us as teachers.

- Allow yourself to teach in any way you want—in any way that feels natural to you—as opposed to modeling someone else's way of teaching.

- Some teachers thrive when they teach in a very organized way, such as using the same sequence each time. This method offers a sense of direction and confidence.

- Similar to the method of simply enjoying yourself, teach poses or a style of yoga that you're passionate about. This relieves stress while building confidence.

- For many, music helps us relax. We can choose to teach with soothing or inspiring music playing in the background.

- By thinking of ourselves as performing artists, rather than yoga teachers or exercise instructors we access a creative perspective on teaching that eases fears. Yoga *is* a healing *art,* after all.

- Finding the keys to setting yourself free as a teacher is the name of the game. It's an intuitive process that each of us will find in our own way, in our own time.

Yandara experience, philosophies, and teachings

Nature is one of our greatest teachers. One of the best things about the Yandara Yoga Institute home center is the location in Baja California Sur, Mexico. You get to experience the miracle of getting up and out of bed and walking to the beach. The Pacific Ocean setting and the quiet calm of the Baja peninsula desert have the ability to renew your entire being after some time spent here. You may feel as if your life has been reset. You might liken the experience to feeling like a child again, experiencing this natural lifestyle for the first time in your life.

At times students report being filled with a sense of wonder and awe as they walk along the beach in between classes or sit in meditation with the sound of waves embracing the sandy shoreline. We encourage everyone to use the sheer magnificence of the Pacific to enhance their experience of simply *being*.

You get to experience a sense of playfulness, aliveness, stillness, and quiet. After greeting the sunrise or taking an early morning meditation practice on the beach, you walk to breakfast and eat in silence. You experience what it's like to eat, to sit, to be around your friends—in silence.

We have many workshops that explore the *behind-the-scenes* principles of yoga—why it works and how it works. While you probably won't end up sharing this information with your students it *will* be something you'll need to know. You'll probably find it becomes something you *enjoy* learning and knowing. Enjoyment is an essential part of the yoga teacher training intensive.

As yoga teachers we typically emulate a feeling or experience given to us by *our* teachers. We see what they did, know what worked for them, and follow in their footsteps—in the hope of getting the same results. We may or may not understand why the way they taught worked so well. We might miss something because we're going through the motions without understanding them. By duplicating what our teacher does we often miss out on some key elements.

When you go through Yandara's teacher training there are two major things happening. First, you're learning specific linear information necessary for teaching. Second, you're aligning with a keen sense of personal empowerment. Both of these experiences are equally important. Your ability to be present, and your ability to be conscious in your heart—while radiating an energy of peace and loving kindness—is as important as any technical knowledge you'll receive.

You did not necessarily come back to your favorite teacher because they were an advanced asana practitioner adept in handstands, arm balances, and other challenging postures, but because there was something inexplicable and attractive about their energy. That's what a yoga class is all about. At Yandara we emphasize the point that your unique energy as an individual is what will draw students to your classes. The seeds of presence and heart-centered living is what you'll plant and grow during your Yandara experience.

So often we fail to comprehend this. An energetic mindset is rarely taught to us in school or by our parents. We are rarely taught to honor and respect this inexplicable quality in a human being. Emphasis is often put on what we *know* and what we *accomplish*. And, of course, the attainment of a certain material lifestyle. Throughout our yoga teacher training we continually touch upon these points in order to evolve as teachers, as well as human beings cultivating a spiritual life.

By the end of a Yandara yoga teacher training you will most likely feel happier and healthier. I want to emphasize this because in our culture we've built up a resistance to feeling good. We're often habituated to complaining and looking for the negative. And we even do this within the dogmatic clicks of the religious institutions our culture celebrates.

Developing your individual spiritual nature through yoga does nothing of the sort. It's a pure form of spirituality unaccompanied by dogma or religion. It's a healing practice that can be taken wherever you want to take it. Whereas religion often promotes following an external form of the divine, yoga supports following the Self. Yoga is a cultivation of knowing who you are, at the deepest level, as opposed to following someone else's beliefs.

In my classes I like to have a student volunteer come up to the front of the class for a martial arts demonstration. Without knowing what I'll ask them to do I give them a gentle push, which surprises them because they weren't expecting it. This is a yoga class, not a martial arts class, right?

The student is typically a bit reactive, and taken aback. Their amygdala may kick in as if to say, *you're in danger.* What I'm doing here is making a point as to how we go about our daily lives. We're so often daydreaming in our heads, lost in past events or future scenarios. If somebody honks their horn or says something that jars us, we feel hurt and totally taken off guard.

Typically, we react in one of two ways: either we're like wisps in the wind, blown around by anyone who yells at us or hurts us and feeling like a victim of circumstances, or we become defensive and aggressive. Instead of calmly saying, *You know, that really hurts,* we say, *Hey you jerk! How dare you! You can't hurt me! I'm tougher than that!* Then the walls of self-preservation go up, because we sure as heck don't want to get hurt again.

The same sort of thing happens in a yoga class and in our role as yoga teachers. I often notice teachers who enter a class feeling insecure and uncertain. Many of us are afraid that someone isn't going to like us or that we're not going to teach as well as we hope. So we either take an aggressive attitude in class in order to take control, or we take the opposite attitude, energetically asking, *Oh, is this all right? Am I doing this right? Am I teaching a good class?*

There is, however, a middle road we're not normally accustomed to following. And I'd like to illustrate it by returning to the exercise in which I push the teacher trainee.

Say, for example, that the student is standing up and I've just pushed him. I say, *Hey there, I'm coming at you again. What are you gonna do?* They brace themselves, thinking I'm going to push them again. Instead, I place my hand very gently on their shoulder. They can't feel it, they're still rigid and aggressively preparing themselves for some sort of attack. They don't feel any inkling of love or warmth.

So, I say to them, *I see that when you freeze up, you have a protective wall around you, energetically speaking, which prevents you from feeling warmth or loving feelings.* It's as if the student has anesthetized themselves. They have numbed themselves so as not to be hurt again.

Then I say, *Okay, let's try it again. Get ready, here I come! Tense up like you did before!* And, they do. And again, I push them. Then I say, *How does that feel*? And inevitably they say, *Well, it actually feels worse than when I was caught off guard. My own resistance caused even more discomfort.*

This is an example of a martial arts demonstration, but it makes sense to bring these energetic principles into our Yandara flow series. The principles of martial arts help us understand, and put into practice, how our body intuitively adapts to what's needed. But we have to break down our protective walls in order to do so, and this can take a while, depending upon what traumas we've experienced and how we've dealt with them. Luckily, yoga helps us break down those barriers.

What if you were extremely conscientious of what was going on in your surroundings? Using the example above, the story would play out like this:

You observe your 'opponent.' Rather than being caught off guard, you feel into the energy of your environment, and can sense an event before it happens, determining whether or not a person or situation is safe. You're seeing clearly, and resting in heart-centered awareness. Your intuition is developed and turned on. You can even predict things before they happen. And, with time, your sixth sense becomes a powerful ally.

When we translate this to our yoga mats it may look something like this:

We stand with a strong foundation—one in which we can't be pushed over. The Yandara standing series includes this stance—where the knees are bent slightly, and the legs are apart, just a bit wider than hips distance. When someone pushes you, you simply move along with it, or you move out of the way, deflecting his or her energy.

This interplay becomes comfortable—playful even. We begin to see the energy in the other person's eyes. When we all sink into this grounded sense of awareness, everybody relaxes into their *being*. We're fluid and flowing rather than rigid and tight. We allow energy to move through us. Life becomes less stressful, and much less threatening. This is the nature of somatic healing, which we experience through yoga.

Many of these principles are better demonstrated in a classroom setting where you can feel the energy in the room. That's what yoga is about. It's about creating an energy field—a space within which to practice moving—in a way that's more harmonious with life. This is one of Yandara's core teachings.

Communication skills

During yoga teacher training we do a lot of different practices centered around communication. Generally speaking, this is about finding and resting in your authentic self and your authentic voice when presenting to a class. Once you've found your authentic voice the energy in the room shifts. It's as if the entire room takes a big, deep breath and—ahhhh—let's it all out. We do lots of exercises during yoga teacher training that help us pinpoint the shifts in energy that occur when we speak with our authentic voices. We look at the energy of the student teacher, as well as how their energy affects us as students.

If you've ever had the pleasure of going to see live theatre or attended any kind of live performance, you may have noticed that one or two performers have an inexplicable life force of energy while others are just so-so. At the time you may not have been able to put your finger on what was happening—but, looking back, you can probably relate to what I'm talking about. Maybe you recall a time when you saw your favorite band and, at one point during the concert, everything came together and it was like—*wow! Magic!* Their authentic selves emerged on the stage and what a beautiful experience it was.

We *all* have this magical presence, and during teacher training we find ways to tap into that presence. In doing so, *you* relax and your *students* relax, because they don't have to play a role anymore either. It's exhausting to wear the mask of the ego—and yet we do it all the time. We come into yoga class, probably feeling a little insecure, and we inadvertently wear that mask.

We might be searching for approval. We might be wondering whether our students will like our teaching style. So many thoughts run through our heads—most of them judgmental. And we do this because we want to teach a good class for our students or we're scared we won't do or say what we'd planned to. Just know that every teacher goes through this and it gets easier with time and practice.

We really want to be like this:

I'm here, just as I am. This is what I know, and this is how I teach.

Some people will like your teaching style and some won't. You might be the best teacher in the entire world—and yet your style just isn't going to jive with some people. And that's okay. That's just the way it is. There's a reason we're all different, and a reason why we resonate with certain people and not others.

One exercise we do during yoga teacher training goes something like this:

I ask a student to come to the front of the class to make a short presentation. I ask them to share with the class their strengths and challenges. This exercise illustrates the point that, most of the time, the reason we're afraid of who we are is that we're afraid of looking either too good or too bad. It goes both ways but, in general, we're afraid of coming off as conceited.

We're afraid our students will be thinking, *Oh, look at her. She's so full of herself.* We're afraid of our greatness, and we're even more afraid of our weaknesses. Wouldn't it be nice if we could just say, *Here's what I'm good at. This is where my life experiences seem to have brought me at this point. I'm fairly efficient in doing this or that. In other areas, I have challenges.*

When students move into a state of self-acceptance we witness a shift of energy that's both therapeutic and beautiful. It's a different kind of paradigm because, most of the time, when we're making presentations, we're creating separation. I'm the teacher. You're the student. If you want to control a class you have to present in a manner that prevents you from losing control. In doing so you put on a certain persona.

Often the issue is that we're afraid of looking pompous or too good. We're afraid of being made a fool of if we don't know the right answer. For example, when we make a minor mistake like forgetting the name of a pose we're teaching or saying, *left leg* when we mean right. But we can make the choice to simply move on without making a big deal about it.

Yoga is about balance. We trust that our students will respond to us in a respectful way. We trust that they will pay attention, follow instructions, and do the work they came to class to do. Most of the time students are in class because they want to be. When this is the case the teacher-student dynamic is different. This special dynamic is enhanced by yoga, not only because both teacher and student choose to be there, but also because yoga ignites a certain authenticity in us all. For teachers *and* students it encourages us to manifest our gifts, drop our egos, and move more deeply into our hearts.

Lesson planning and themes

Creating a theme for your yoga class takes it to an entirely new level and sets it apart from other classes. When selecting a theme for your class always choose something you're drawn to. Perhaps you love to bring elements of nature into your classes—like a full moon flow, for example. Or maybe you're interested in philosophy. So you pick a lesson from Patanjali's Yoga Sutras and weave that lesson throughout your class. If you're into the theme your students will like it too.

Also, you'll probably want to choose a theme that resonates with most people. You won't want to create an entire class around an obscure Hindu deity without explaining what they represent. A universal feeling like joy, or playfulness can make a good theme for a class. Balance and equanimity are popular themes. You might use the theme of balance in asanas as a metaphor for life. When life gets sticky do we collapse or maintain a sense of balance? You could ask your students to ponder this question as you guide them in and out of balancing poses.

If you're a lover of poetry you may wish to recite a poem at the beginning of class and then read it again while your students are resting in savasana. You may even make copies of the poem to hand out after class. As you grow as a teacher you'll likely find that weaving themes into your classes lends to endless creativity, and therefore greater inspiration for your students. Many themes are timeless and can be integrated into your classes over and over again. You might keep coming back to a handful of themes because they resonate with you and your students. That's perfectly okay.

We've talked a lot about finding one's edge, which is constantly changing from one day to the next. This is one of those timeless themes you may continually focus on because it's such a simple yet profound principle. The edge happens when resistance comes rushing in—be it physical, mental, or emotional.

The cool thing about our edge is that it spotlights our habitual, unconscious patterns, and our yoga mat is the perfect place to play with this physical and psychological edge because it's safe. When we take our students into a pose and they come to their edge, rather than push them beyond it we teach them how to relax *into* it. We have them use their breath, soften their gaze, and develop a sense of awareness and acceptance around it.

The one word theme is another simple yet beautiful way to theme a class. Words such as enjoyment, attention, ground, harmony, expand, resilience, surrender, balance, and stillness are all powerful words that offer limitless possibilities for theming inspirational classes.

I like to use the theme of enjoyment. With this particular theme we really tune into the feeling of joy in our bodies as we lead our students through postures. We can move our students in a way that feels like they're dancing with such enjoyment they're not even aware of the workout their bodies are receiving.

When I surf, I'm in such a state of joyous flow I don't even notice what an incredible workout I've had for the hour or so that I've been playing with the waves. I'm wrapped up in excitement and total presence. There's tension, strength, and a fluidity of movement in surfing that takes me to a dimension of sheer enjoyment. We can do the same when we teach yoga. Our classes can be playful, light, and full of joy.

Again, when choosing a one word theme, meditate upon what words deeply inspire you. When you're inspired, your students will be too. Working with themes takes practice, so be patient and gentle with yourself. If you feel that sticking to a theme is too challenging or feels constrictive in any way, don't worry about it.

A couple of things to learn in terms of sequencing are:

- How to make adjustments once you have a good grasp of the underlying principles behind all the sequences.
- How to make adjustments once you have a good grasp of the four primary forms of yogic movement.

Once you really understand this, as well as reflex mechanisms like the stretch reflex and the clasp-knife reflex, you'll be able to easily adapt your classes to create safe and effective yoga sequences.

Many years ago I was asked to teach a yoga class to a group of four elderly meditators. Their basic range of motion was limited and involved being able to only bend forward a few inches. How was I going to teach them an effective yoga class? The prospect seemed challenging, to say the least. So I spontaneously designed a simple class.

We sat in chairs, gently twisting from one side to the next. We swayed our bodies and rolled our wrists and ankles. We did basic movements. They all enjoyed themselves and experienced a lovely introduction to yoga. None of them felt daunted or intimidated by it because we moved gently—through classic yoga poses with modifications suitable for their bodies.

Was this even yoga? Once you fully understand yoga's underlying principles you can answer with an emphatic *yes!* Creating a yoga class for any level—from the complete beginner to the advanced student—will come naturally and easily to you.

Safety

The key element in safety is teaching the students how to be consciously aware of their bodies.

This is surprising but true. A lot of people don't know what pain is because they're not in touch with their bodies. They're only in their heads, mainly identifying with their thoughts. They do yoga poses because their teacher and peers in the yoga class are doing them, even if these poses are causing pain. Once in the pose they think, *wait, I don't want to be doing this, but so and so next to me is doing it and...*

Then they get injured.

This is why it's your job to teach your students how to become deeply embodied and deeply in touch with their sensations. As soon as there's pain they need to know it's time to back off.

Let's take an example. A yoga practitioner was a very precise yoga student, having trained in the Iyengar method for years. Iyengar yoga is a style known for its emphasis on precision, alignment, and safety. This works for the majority of people but because some people's bodies are structurally different the same guidelines may not apply. Everyone's bodies are different.

During class one day they were practicing downward facing dog and performing it perfectly—according to the alignment principles of Iyengar Yoga. However, this particular yoga practitioner wasn't paying attention to the painful sensations in their body. Instead, they ignored them. *No, I'm doing the pose correctly,* they thought. But they weren't—not for their particular body. And they weren't listening to the sensations. Instead, they listened to external cues of alignment. And, of course, they ended up injuring their back.

The best way to keep your students safe is by teaching them how to really know and listen to their body's sensations—how to find their personal edge and work from there.

Intention

I believe that a person's deepest intentions—those that spring forth from one's inner wisdom—are the forces that shape our destiny. And when we bring positive intentions to our classes they become that much more effective.

Before setting an intention for class or asking your students to set their own intention, sit quietly in stillness for a few moments. You could begin by guiding them through a simple seated meditation or pranayama technique. This allows us time to drop out of the chatter of our minds and into the gap of expanded awareness. It's in this place of our higher self where intentions flourish.

An intention might be dedicating our practice to someone we love—someone in need of healing energy. We might offer up our practice to the health and safety of all living beings.

As a teacher you may want to suggest that students feel into one value they'd like to bring more of into their lives—for example, trust, love, freedom, truth, compassion or wisdom—these are all excellent examples of one word intentions.

The thing that gives an intention its power is how strongly it's connected to our true selves. The most powerful intentions reside deep within—like a seed planted in the heart, with all the potential to burst forth into material reality. We can more effortlessly achieve what we want when our intentions flow from our hearts.

Our deepest intentions work to make us whole and more complete. The evolutionary force that surrounds us supports these heartfelt intentions. These heartfelt intentions are not constrained by past conditioning or past traumas. The more we guide our students to drop into their hearts and into unbounded awareness the more they get to know their true selves. What an amazing gift to give our students! When we really know ourselves—at the core of our being—we become powerful yogis able to manifest our most heartfelt desires and intentions.

We also need intention regarding the postures we teach our students, as well as the ones we practice at home. Students sometimes ask me if they're doing a particular pose right. My answer is always, *it depends on what part of the body you want to affect, and your intention behind the pose.* Small adjustments make profound changes in the body. Maybe you want to strengthen the legs or work the core muscles. Or maybe your intention is to open the hips. There's nothing right or wrong, either way. It's just a different pose depending upon your intention and what part of the body you want to impact.

Notice how your experience of life shifts when you bring intention to it. The intention could be an overarching theme—to be more mindful, for instance. If this were the case, you would practice mindfulness in everything you do—whether it's putting on a pair of shoes, cooking breakfast, or having a conversation with a friend. In fact, why don't you experiment with the intention of mindful listening? The next time you're having a conversation, let the mind quiet and drop into your heart space as you chat. See what it feels like to really *listen* to the other person without constantly *thinking* about how you are going to respond. The conversation may feel slower than usual, but you'll be connecting on a more intimate level.

You might bring another kind of intention to your life and, hence, your teaching. The intention could be one of seeing *everything* as divinity. Every anxious thought, every interaction (seemingly good or bad), every sound (however harsh, sweet, soft, or jarring)—everything is regarded as divine. Even your fears, for they too, are showing you something innately human about yourself. This is a powerful way to go about life, and one that will transform your experience by leaps and bounds.

Intention truly is *everything*.

The modern day dilemma

There's a dilemma in the world of yoga today that I'd like to touch upon here. When I began practicing yoga there was a simplicity to it that no longer exists. Teachers weren't trained in anatomy and physiology—nor were the yogis who came from India to teach us. They just *knew* that the ways they moved their bodies had deep and lasting effects.

To put it simply, yoga worked. True, many elements of safety were lacking but, all in all, the ancient ways were sound. As we took classes from these yogis very few hurt themselves because we were learning to be conscious of the sensations in our bodies throughout the entire process.

Now that the Western mind is involved there's an entirely new school of thought when it comes to teaching yoga. Now you're expected to be not just a yoga teacher but almost a physical therapist too. The line between yoga and yoga therapy isn't always clear, however. The extensive anatomy and physiology required in many yoga teacher trainings is not nearly enough to make you a physical therapist.

It takes five or six years to become a physical therapist with credentials to work in the field. You can't be expected, as a 200-hour yoga teacher, to know everything you need to know about anatomy and physiology, or even yoga therapy. It's beyond the scope of a 200-hour program—and yet, it's stressful when you don't know these things.

Unfortunately this may lead to some yoga teachers pretending to know things they don't.

Why?

Because there's a lot of pressure to have all the answers in terms of anatomy and physiology, and the function of the physical body. As a beginning yoga teacher one of your students might approach you after class saying, *I have pain in this joint. What should I do about it?* Or, *Why do my feet cramp so much in balancing poses?* So you answer spontaneously, with the best of intentions, without really knowing the solution from an expert's point of view.

As you can see, we have a bit of a dilemma here. In my opinion we should determine where to draw the line. In a 200-hour teacher training you need the information necessary to become a good yoga teacher, not a yoga therapist. Which begs a question many prospective yoga teachers ask themselves:

How can you learn everything you need to know in 200 hours?

At Yandara, we're teaching you basic principles needed to safely increase the life force energy within your students. This is different from yoga therapy. So when someone asks you, *What do I do with this lower back injury*? You simply say, *I'm a hatha yoga teacher. You should seek help from a physical therapist or a trained yoga therapist.*

It's better to be clear about your level of competency than to stress yourself out, or even cause injury because you don't really know the answers. A lot of people I talk to who are super sharp in their yoga practice don't really know what's going on deep inside the body. *I* know the basic principles we've been exploring in this book because I've been practicing and teaching yoga for such a long time. But even I don't know the specifics in terms of anatomy and physiology. I was never trained as a physical therapist—or even a yoga therapist, for that matter. But I *do* know when yoga teachers come up with explanations in an attempt to help their students without really having the information at hand.

One reason we exercise is because it's relaxing. The reason so many people can't receive the blissful, loving energy that pervades life, is because they're walking around in a chronic state of stress. And they don't even know it. It's easy to become accustomed to such a state—and many of us are. In a feeling of rigidity, you can't receive. Think of the many times you've walked outside and yet you can't really appreciate how beautiful the clouds are or how beautiful the wind is, because you're living in your head. The mind is mostly stress-oriented.

Why?

Because the function of the brain is to protect us from dangerous elements. But, the worry that ensues is inherently stressful. As yoga teachers, we want to teach our students how to alleviate that stress and create an optimized flow of prana.

So how do we do that? How do we move a person's body in order to create the maximum flow of life force energy?

It's important to remember that we're creating a flow of energy through the blood vessels, through the nerves, and through the nadis (or meridians). Stress constricts the flow of energy. So our primary job as yoga teachers is to reduce stress in our students' bodies.

This is one of the main reasons your students return to your yoga class again and again. Because you reduce their stress levels with each class. They feel so much better by the time savasana rolls around. What's more, you have loads of relaxation techniques in your yoga teacher toolbox to offer your students. These techniques go far beyond the outdated way someone might have said to you in the past, *just relax*. For someone in a state of deep stress, this does nothing. But you have the knowledge to help this deeply stressed out yoga student.

Bringing the yoga elixir back home

If you've ever studied the mythological insights of Joseph Campbell you're probably familiar with *The Hero's Journey.* If you don't have a clue as to what I'm talking about, let me give you a brief explanation.

The Hero's Journey is an observation of the principles that shape the conduct of a fully human life, as well as the concepts and stages that repeatedly appear in many of the myths and stories that involve heroes and adventure.

If you've ventured out of your ordinary life to attend an intensive yoga teacher training you're no doubt on one of these life journeys, and it stands to reason that this particular journey—if you take a good look at it—embodies some of the various stages of the archetypal *Hero's Journey.*

To delve deeper into this world, you'll want to read Joseph Campbell's *The Hero with a Thousand Faces.* But, in a nutshell, the stages look like this:

The Ordinary World—The Call to Adventure—Refusal of the Call—Mentor—Crossing the First Threshold—Tests, Allies, and Enemies—

Approach to the Innermost Cave—The Ordeal—Reward—The Road Back—Resurrection—Return with the Elixir.

Many Hollywood films, bestselling novels, or fables and myths involving characters undertaking a challenging journey or experience reflect these stages. Furthermore, looking at the chapters and stories of your own life, you may recognize many of these stages—particularly the chapter of your becoming a yoga teacher.

Study your journey to undertaking a yoga teacher training and I have no doubt you'll find parallels which speak to your own hero's journey. It's no small feat to do what you're doing.

You are the hero of your own journey.

Your story began at home, in your *Ordinary World*, where you felt *The Call to Adventure*—the call to change your life and become a yoga teacher, or at least to deepen your practice and transform your relationship to yoga. You may have *Refused the Call*, because you were scared. This stage is always about fear and it's totally normal. Your mind may have come up with a million excuses as to why this whole yoga teacher training thing was a bad idea.

But then, a *Mentor* in some shape or form came into your life and confirmed the longing you'd had to do something new and change. Your mentor might have been a close friend who encouraged you to go, or perhaps even a sign from the Universe that your eyes were open enough to see. Mentors come in many shapes and sizes, as do heroes—hence the title of Campbell's book, 'The Hero with a *Thousand* Faces.'

As you *Crossed the First Threshold* your plane took off—the ship's whistle blew—you were bound for whatever unfamiliar destination would serve as the backdrop for your training. The destination was across the globe, on the beaches of Mexico—or in your own backyard at a local yoga studio. No matter, you were on your way, and there was no turning back.

Your yoga teacher training has no doubt *Tested* you. It's an intensive experience after all, taking you out of your comfort zone and forcing you to leave familiar habits behind. It brings you *Allies* in the form of new friends and teachers. It also manifests *enemies* in the form of your shadows and those parts of yourself you never dared look at. But, within the safe space of your training, the wounds and scars you have carried in your body and mind for many years bubbled up to the surface for healing.

Mentors, Tests, Allies, and Enemies come in all forms, shapes, and sizes. And, you often don't realize what face they wore until you reflect back upon your journey some time later.

Chances are, you'll make the spiritual journey to your *Innermost Cave* to meet whatever is awaiting. You'll live to tell the tale, but may experience a rather challenging *Ordeal* along the way. The *Reward*—the yoga elixir you'll hold in the palm of your consciousness—makes it all worthwhile as you begin traveling your *Road Back* home.

The journey back home may have its own share of obstacles as you deal with post-training blues, trying to make sense of it all. You have been transformed, after all, and may need to experience the stage known as the *Resurrection*. This particular stage marks the final challenge: you have the magical elixir—the reward of the knowledge and experience of your yoga training—and yet there's still a hurdle. A final exam of sorts that you must take before returning home with the elixir. In yoga teacher training this might play out during the final teaching sessions.

At Yandara, we always have *teach outs* in the last days of the teacher training programs. Teach outs often revolve around a 15-minute teaching slot in which you put everything you've learned into action.

This might prove challenging. We prepare our students well, and provide a loving, non-judgmental space where everyone can be vulnerable. But this doesn't mean it's easy. However, you may find that you enjoy the opportunity to put everything you have learned into practice one final time before heading back out into the world, *Returning with the Elixir*, and beginning to share it with others.

And here we are, at the end of this particular end of the journey—and, no doubt, at the beginning of another.

May each and every one of you go and share your teachings with the world. Spread peace, spread health, and spread love. This is what yoga is all about. And you are the teacher who will share this with everyone you meet.

Made in USA - Kendallville, IN
94967_9780986494529
12.22.2022 1344